Claiming Your Self-Esteem

A Guide Out of Codependency, Addiction, and Other Useless Habits.

Claiming Your Self-Esteem

A Guide Out of Codependency, Addiction, and Other Useless Habits

by Carolyn M. Ball

CELESTIALARTS

Berkeley, California

The author gratefully acknowledges permission to reprint excerpts from Advice From A Failure, *by Jo Courdert, copyright © 1965, originally published by Stein & Day, Inc., reprinted with permission of Scarborough House Publishers.*

Cover design by Julie Mulvaney

PUBLISHED IN ASSOCIATION WITH ARATI BOOKS, HOUSTON, TEXAS.

Library of Congress Cataloging in Publication Data

Ball, Carolyn M.
　　　Claiming your self-esteem : a guide out of codependency, addiction, and other useless habits / by Carolyn M. Ball.
　　　　　p.　　cm.
　　　Includes bibliographical references.
　　　ISBN 0-89087-645-2
　　　1. Codependents—Rehabilitation.　2. Compulsive behavior.　3. Self-respect.　I. Title.
RC569.5.C63B35　1991
158'.1—dc20　　　　　　　　　　　　　　　　　　　　　90-24633
　　　　　　　　　　　　　　　　　　　　　　　　　　　　CIP

6 7 8 9 10 — 01 00 99 98 97

This book is dedicated

to my father and mother, William and Dorothy Matthias, with gratitude for all their devotion and unconditional love,

to my Teacher, Mary Thunder, whose spiritual guidance has been the cornerstone of all my growth in these past years,

to Brad Brown, translator extraordinaire of the Truth into language and processes which people can use and understand,

and to Shellie Newell, my dear, dear friend, who has walked with me through all these changes and much, much more.

A special thank you

To William and Dorothy Matthias, Katherine Park, Shellie Newell, Martin Rastall, Bill Perry, Joe Vitale, Bill Ball, Joe Montgomery, Mike Yeaman, Vicki Redd, Phyllis Gruver, Ann Tripp, and Julie Mulvaney for your skilled and insightful contributions and feedback on the contents and concepts of this book; to Ann Skotty for your computer expertise; to Ed McGinnis and Ron Kaye for allowing me to pass on your original material; to Shakti Miller for showing me my codependency; and to Brad Brown and Roy Whitten, founders of the Life Training which taught me so much more about human growth than my formal education ever could.

Contents

Preface

This book addresses the most important thing we can give ourselves: self-esteem. For most of my life I have worked in the area of personal growth-- sometimes from a psychological perspective, sometimes from a spiritual perspective. But somehow simple and genuine happiness remained illusive to me until a major crisis took place which finally showed me a pattern painfully common among human beings: that when we do not love and value ourselves, we participate in codependent, addictive, and compulsive habits in order to feel good--to give ourselves a sense of self-esteem. What happens instead, however, is that these patterns actually perpetuate, and are symptoms of, low self-esteem.

Without the knowledge, high regard, and acceptance of ourselves that are the foundation of true self-esteem, we do not know how to care for ourselves properly nor create what we want and need in our lives. When things are not going the way we want, when we're on the downward spiral, when we've made mistakes, or when we're criticized or ostracized--do we become our own best friend? Are we gentle and loving with ourselves? Not at all. We add our own insults to the injuries we have already experienced, mercilessly berate ourselves, and in essence, are the first to abandon our own ships.

We are not in a culture that teaches us to love ourselves *unconditionally*. It teaches us that we are lovable only *if* we look good, are wealthy, and produce perfectly a lot of profitable widgets. Thus we learn that love is not only conditional, but it is conditional upon standards to which we can almost never measure up. Despite our best efforts, we all get old, spend our money, and continue to discover that our perfect widgets, in time, lose their glamour.

In recent years several wealthy American communities have been devastated by the shock of multiple teen suicides. "But we've given them everything! What have we done wrong?" The agony of things going so wrong when we thought we'd done it all right is beyond words. Sadly, it is often the most painful experiences that awaken us to the changes we need to make in our lives. Perhaps the most important such change is to redirect our attention to the hearts and minds of our fellow humans and ourselves. With all the benefits our society provides, one that has been lost along the way is the inner knowing that each of us has inherent value, apart from what we do, what we have, and what we produce. We are not human doings; we are human beings.

I spent a good part of my childhood in Brazil. I think it was there that I got my first clues about the nature of self-esteem. There is a level of poverty there that is barely seen at all in the United States. I would watch the children play near the tin lean-tos they called home. Some of the children were pitifully skinny, some were actually naked--but they would laugh, and run, and take care of each other as if the world were filled with nothing but comfort. Their eyes were full of joy and delight. They had so little, and yet they were happy! The values of that culture were even reflected in the faces of the poor; each child seemed to have his dignity, a sense of himself that was beyond his external conditions.

Yet in our culture we often have esteem or value for ourselves because of our possessions and what we produce. But this is not true self-esteem. The word *esteem* is defined as "high regard." To have *self-esteem* is to have respect, admiration and a high value of ourselves; it is unconditional. When we speak of low self-esteem, we are referring to a low regard or value of ourselves. When we have *low self-esteem,* we often value ourselves only under certain conditions.

When our self-esteem is low, we attempt to compensate with certain behaviors that give us *artificial* self-esteem. We fill the emptiness created by our lack of self-worth with *codependent* relationships. A codependent relationship is one which is compulsive and mutually dependent in an unhealthy manner. We feel we *need* it, that we are not okay without it. While codependency is generally considered to be an addictive relationship to other people, I am suggesting here that we actually develop exactly the same kind of relationship with work, food, alcohol, drugs, and other substances and behaviors. Consequently, when I speak of codependency in this book, it should be kept in mind that the same principles apply to other compulsive and addictive patterns. Codependency says, in essence, "Since I don't have any innate value, I'll act and look a certain way if you (spouse, career, alcohol) will make me feel good about myself." Of course it never works well, but we can persist in the illusion for a lifetime.

When I was in graduate school, I discovered there was pitifully little written about self-esteem and almost nothing about how to help a client raise his self-esteem. When I researched the subject, I found that the word "self-esteem" was not even listed in the

Library of Congress Catalogue, (although "self-defense" and "self-denial" were heartily catalogued). It was not addressed *once* in *any* of my classes. Yet, I was at the time, and am still convinced that low self-esteem lies at the core of most human unhappiness. Later, as I worked in the field of codependency and addiction, I noticed that low self-esteem was considered a symptom of those dysfunctions. But as I have led groups, taught classes, and counseled one-on-one, I have observed over and over again that the reverse is true; *codependency and addiction are, in fact, symptoms of low self-esteem. People turn to those compulsive behaviors when they feel empty inside and want to feel better about themselves.* Hence these issues are intimately connected; we cannot heal one without addressing the other.

Each person is unique and special. All of us have our own gifts to give as we pass through life on this planet. When we are in touch with ourselves--who we are, what we feel, what we need, what we love and enjoy--then that special gift can be expressed. When life is full of "have-tos" and "shoulds" and trying to measure up to external standards, it is impossible to be in touch with ourselves or that inner gift. They become obscured by the busy-ness of trying to be different from how we are. But, by honoring ourselves exactly as we are, the bad with the good, that inner gift is brought back to the forefront and is allowed expression. The net effect is the same whether our perspective is from a psychological framework and is called self-esteem, or from a spiritual framework and is called Higher Self, Higher Power, or the God Within.

This book illuminates the missing link between low self-esteem and the codependent thoughts and behaviors that create it. It also provides the much needed shift in perspective from, "You need self-esteem" to "This is how to achieve self-esteem." It offers both insight into how and why we get into nonbeneficial patterns, and the tools for extricating ourselves. It shows us how to be at home inside ourselves.

Chapter One explains the relationship between self-esteem and codependency. Chapters Two and Three show how self-esteem can be undermined by habitual thoughts, or "old programs," and the technology for putting it back together. Chapter Four discusses the typical codependent patterns resulting from those programs and how we use them to create a false sense of self-esteem. Chapters Five and Six consider why we inadvertently *keep* our old codependent behaviors long after they have served us, and how to get off that treadmill. Chapters Seven, Eight and Nine address our *real* selves: who we are when we pull out all the stops and play out our lives to the fullest. They demonstrate how we can have a healthy relationship with ourself and how we can have truly intimate, and fulfilling, relationships with others.

I want to say to each reader: "THIS IS YOUR LIFE!" You can read through this book, put it on the shelf with your other self-help books, and continue to beat yourself up because you aren't the way you want to be. Or, you can take the messages contained within these pages and apply them to your life. You can do the exercises, and make the shifts that will help you live your life in a way that is exciting, interesting and fun *because you are in touch with yourself, because you love unconditionally the most important person in your life--YOU.*

1

What Self-Esteem Is and What It Isn't

DISCOVERING SELF-ESTEEM

Once, some years back, I had the job of my dreams. I was working for an exciting, progressive foundation which offered workshops in personal growth and development. It was the kind of position one can scarcely believe exists. It used all of my skills, was always interesting and exciting, and had boundless opportunities for creative expansion. After having done volunteer work for two years, I was offered an administrative position. I was ecstatic.

Five months later, a new director was brought in. During the shuffling I was offered an opportunity to transfer to any one of several other major cities in which the foundation had offices. But the new director asked me to stay, saying she had much to learn from me. My codependent need to be seen as helpful won out over intuition. Within a week I was relocated at a reception desk in the front. My counseling and administrative functions were assigned to someone else. I was essentially ignored. Helpless, I watched the growing evidence that my presence was no longer needed nor wanted. I tried several times to make appointments with the new director and other administrators to discuss the situation. Each attempt seemed to get short-circuited.

I hit a level of depression I had rarely experienced before. All that I had worked for in the past years was slipping away from me. I remember sitting by the large picture window next to my desk, staring out at the three-story building across the parking lot and wondering if a plunge from the rooftop would have a net result of ending my pain--or if I'd just break a leg and make it worse. I wondered if, in fact, there were any stairs to the roof, or if one would have to buy a ladder. My mind ran rampant.

The final blow was not a surprise. At four o'clock Friday afternoon, with only enough time to gather my personal possessions, I was given my final paycheck--no severence pay, no exit interview or explanation--and told I was being let go. "Some people just aren't cut out for this kind of work," I was told. My world crumbled.

Although I could not know it at the time, this event was to be a great blessing in disguise--perhaps the greatest of my life. But at the time I wanted to die. I was bitter. I was lost. I had no idea how to put it all back together. I blamed myself for not being good enough. If I was not cut out for the work I loved, what was there to live for? I told myself that I was useless and that I would never be able to do the kind of work that was meaningful to me, that I was powerless, had no social skills, and I was a waste of space on this planet. I accused myself of having something basically wrong with me, and for being stupid because I couldn't figure out what that was.

That weekend I rented a truck, threw all my stuff in it, headed the two thousand miles back home, and began the slow process of healing. In the weeks and months that followed, as I started putting the pieces back together, I gradually became aware that the devastation I had felt had not so much been from the negative experiences I'd had, but from how I had *interpreted* them. People have bad things happen to them all the time, I thought. Politics, wars, abuse, loss of jobs and loved ones, poverty--this is all a part of the human experience. How could some people survive, even feel at peace, while others--like myself--want to die?

I thought about the things I'd told myself when I lost my job--that I was useless, that I couldn't do the kind of work I wanted, that I was powerless, that there was something basically wrong with me. I realized none of these things were true. I recognized that even though one director had not appreciated me, there was still an enormous amount of data that said I *was* good at my work. I had seen exciting changes in the clients and had received countless acknowledgments from many quarters. Yet I was remembering none of that; I was focusing only on the pain of rejection. What soon became evident was that when things didn't go the way I wanted, *I had abandoned myself.* I had said some very negative and untrue things to myself and *I* had believed them. In essence, I was experiencing *low self-esteem!* In other words, I was not valuing *me!*

When I realized that I had been very critical and hard on myself, I decided to be gentle and kind to myself instead. I took long walks in the woods and many bubble baths. I began spending time with people who were very supportive of me. I started to listen to the "still, small voice" inside, to honor and respect my own inner direction and promptings, and to rely on what felt right for me instead of what other people thought I should do and be.

In other words, I discovered what it was like to be at home inside of myself. I began a mental and emotional redocorating process that made living inside of me a pleasure instead of a struggle. I became clear that I needed to shift my focus from my failures to my successes. I returned to graduate school, got those magic letters behind my name, and began to live my life as I had always dreamed but had heretofore told myself was impossible.

IDENTIFYING SELF-ESTEEM

What had been the source of devastation became the seeds of a new me. I began to see the events surrounding the loss of my "perfect" job as the stepping stones to realizing perhaps the single most important truth in my life, something I have shared with thousands since. It is the basic belief we have about ourselves when we have self-esteem: *no matter what happens to me or around me, no matter what others may think of me or what I do, I can always love and value myself.* As I looked at the many human situations that we all must face, as I examined the many human behaviors that we all have, I began to recognize that low self-esteem lies at the root of *most* emotional problems. In fact, according to Virginia Satir (1983), a positive view of the self is the very foundation of mental health.

Today I teach workshops on self-esteem, sharing with others what I have learned about valuing and respecting ourselves unconditionally. One of the first things we look at is the type of situations in which we experience the lack of self-esteem. In other words, when do we start telling ourselves we are not good enough? It is always a surprise for people to realize that low self-esteem occurs for them in situations and circumstances that are very similar to those of other people. Usually, low self-esteem is experienced at times when we have not lived up to our own expectations or those of the people around us. We don't accept our own shortcomings and mistakes. We judge ourselves or we are afraid that others will judge us in some way for our limitations.

There are many areas of our lives where low self-esteem may be evident. In relationships we will often experience low self-esteem when we have arguments or disagreements. Sometimes we question our own opinions and think our own views are less valid than those of others. Sometimes we even question our sanity. We often think of ourselves as "less" when we compare ourselves to others and see them as "more"-- more intelligent, wealthier, better looking, healthier, happier, or more whatever. We think of ourselves as "bad" when we behave in a manner that is not up to the standards we have set for ourselves, or when another person appears to treat us poorly. No matter how much we do, we tend to judge ourselves as being "insufficient" if we have not been a Mother Theresa to our friends, lovers, or family. Further, when we do not get what we want, we tell ourselves we are not deserving, that we could have done more, or that we are simply inadequate.

In the world of work, our value is often tied to how much money we make, what kind of office we have, what kind of car we drive, or how much power we can wield. Raises and promotions become a measure of our worth. We tend to measure our worth by how much we produce or how successful we are; and, of course, there is much reinforcement for this viewpoint in the business world. If we are not a smashing success, then we tell ourselves we are a failure.

In our health and physical appearance we are also greatly influenced by external input, in particular from advertising and fashion magazines. We compare ourselves to 19-year-old models who are borderline anorexic, and call ourselves all kinds of nasty things: too old, too weak, decrepit, ugly, stupid, a slob, a pig, and a reject. We describe ourselves as having thunderthighs, elephant knees, rhinocerous skin, cellulite legs, and a coathook for a nose.

In our family life, our love life, our friendships, our career, our sexuality, our appearance, or in the physical, emotional, intellectual, and spiritual aspects of our lives, we are constantly judging ourselves and comparing ourselves to others. Sometimes this self-criticism was learned long ago when we were young. Sometimes we judge ourselves when things don't go the way we would like. At other times we simply adopt the criticisms or standards of others. In all of these cases, we lose our self-esteem when we decide that we are not acceptable the way we are.

✳What is important to understand here is that *self-esteem, or the valuing of oneself, is based on beliefs*. What we *think* or *believe* about ourselves is what determines self-esteem. When there is low self-esteem, there is the belief that "I am not good enough." This is usually accompanied by negative *feelings*, which are the *result* of the thoughts and beliefs (Ellis, 1975). Typical feelings associated with thoughts of "not being good enough" are hurt, depression, anxiety, frustration, anger, and most often, *shame*.

Shame is that painful empty feeling that accompanies low self-esteem. Sometimes it also has a quality of anger directed toward ourselves. There is much currently being written about shame, for it is the emotion that many come to feel when growing up in a dysfunctional or alcoholic family where the child can never be enough or do enough to rectify an impossible situation. Charles Whitfield (1987) says in *Healing the Child Within,* that when we feel shame, we feel hopeless, unforgivable, defective, inadequate and isolated. Shame is the core feeling that results from believing we are not inherently worthwhile.

If low self-esteem is based on variations of the belief that "I am not good enough," then obviously sound self-esteem is based on the belief that "I *am* good enough." True self-esteem is not based on situation or performance. It says, "I am good enough even when I make mistakes and perform poorly; I value myself even when others don't." This is *not* to say that we do not continue to work on ourselves and evolve; it simply means that we continue to have self-esteem through the valleys as well as the peaks of life. To have self-esteem means to think *and* feel as if one has innate, inherent value that does not depend on behavior or external circumstance. *Self-esteem is to unconditionally believe you have high value and unconditionally feel love for yourself.*

SELF-ESTEEM AND CODEPENDENCY: BELIEFS AND HABITS

What losing my "perfect job" taught me was that I could love and respect myself no matter what. Yet it was not until two years later that I discovered in a very personal way another important part of the puzzle: habits. I learned that it is not sufficient to believe we have value. It is also necessary to root out the habitual thought and behavior patterns that keep us from fully experiencing our self-esteem.

The big vision for my life had long been to work in a counseling and healing capacity, in a beautiful country environment, and in cooperation with other professionals in the healing arts. When school was over, I launched my career in that direction. Nothing seemed to hold me back. I was also in a relationship with a dynamic and exciting man who seemed to fit perfectly into my picture of the future. After working for a year as a therapist, I was offered a position that I imagined would catapult me into my dream. It clearly would be the ideal precursor to my success. And it was, but not in the way I thought.

It was another "save the world" job, although I wasn't aware that such was a pattern for me at the time. I was to create and direct a new service facility that was funded by a grant and would be staffed by volunteers. The only hitch was that it had to be running in a month. Similar programs had taken a year or two to become operational, but what a challenge! I was the type who, if someone said it couldn't be done, would roll up my sleeves and say, "Oh, yeah?"

I worked day and night. But soon problems started cropping up. There were countless committees and individuals whose conflicting opinions needed to be taken into consideration. Agreements about the building and furnishings were broken. Volunteers sometimes did not show up. Then it became clear that the designers of the program had not sufficiently studied the need and that we were targeting the wrong population. As the days passed, I started to lose my grip. I leaned very heavily on the man in my life for support, requiring him to bolster me up, give me advice, provide massages for my exhausted body, and to offer constant sympathy for my situation. In the meantime, I tried to perform every needed function to meet the one-month deadline.

At the end of the week that the Center opened (and it opened on schedule), I went home and threw up for five hours. I could not stomach the thought of ever returning to that job again. I was *burned out!* I called up and resigned. But I felt terrible. I had abandoned the people who needed me. I had enough self-esteem to know that I had done my best under nearly impossible conditions, but that didn't make me feel better. I felt like a failure. I turned to the man in my life to lick my wounds. I was grouchy, angry, weepy. "Make me feel better! Tell me it was OK to quit!" But he was burned out, too. I had used him up. He told me he didn't want to see me any more.

My God, I thought, what happened? How could a person with years of introspection and inner work, a person with a masters degree, for goodness sake, blow it--*again?* I thought I had already learned my lessons! What were the missing pieces to this puzzle that were so invisible to me? I didn't feel like dying this time, but the anguish of not knowing how I had gotten into this situation was just as great.

At least I knew this time to be gentle with myself. I stayed with some very loving people. I meditated, prayed, took saunas, and treated myself to dinner out. Then, as I was descibing what had happened to one of my friends, she looked at me and said, "You have to read *Codependent No More*. That's what's going on for you." I'd heard of codependency--like being addicted to a relationship--but really, I'd done too much work on myself to be in any addictive patterns, I was sure. However, something in my gut said--*get that book*.

✳ I read *Codependent No More*, by Melodie Beattie (1987). I was both excited and appalled. There was a list nine pages long that detailed codependent characteristics and behaviors. They included things like: taking responsibility for others, trying to fix and change people, not taking responsiblity for one's own needs or feelings, depending on other people's opinions to feel good about oneself, overcommitting, being a workaholic, eating compulsively, and many, many more. Most of them were uncomfortably familiar. I saw a lifelong pattern of using both my jobs and my relationships in a codependent way so that I could see myself as valuable and important. Codependency was obviously another aspect of self-esteem that I hadn't noticed. We not only believe things about ourselves that give us low self-esteem, but we develop patterns of behavior based on those beliefs that further perpetuate the low self-esteem. In other words, we undermine our sense of self-worth with what we habitually *think* and *do*.

I felt somehow foolish and gullible, that I had spent so many years in patterns that were so easily identifiable, and that I had managed to spend years in psychology without having ever seen this material that was having such an impact on me right now. Yet I was thrilled to finally see a key to the blind spots that had remained so unaffected by my previous self-esteem work.

I immediately began educating myself on addictive behavior. I attended meetings at Codependents Anonymous, Alcoholics Anonymous, Adult Children of Alcholics, Overeaters Anonymous and other similar programs. I took classes and read avidly. What amazed me was that a whole realm of emotional healing work had developed, not through the normal channels of psychology and education, but through the powerful introspective spiritual work of the 12-Step Programs. In addition to programs for alcoholics and their families, these 12-Step Programs serve people who compulsively use drugs, food, sex, gambling, child abuse, work, and of course, relationships. They provide a safe and powerful support system for growth. And what I found to be so special about the 12-Step Programs was that they show people specific and identifiable behavior patterns that are dysfunctional, and steps for creating a healthy lifestyle.

PUTTING IT ALL TOGETHER

As I began healing this second big loss, I had much more material with which to work. For years I had been weighed down with the frustration of not knowing the cause of repeated painful patterns in my life. Now, two important pieces of the puzzle were clear. Now I knew 1) to be aware of the negative thoughts and criticisms of myself, to instead be gentle and kind to myself; and 2) to be aware of the typical behavior habits or patterns into which I had often fallen. In other words, it was important to address the self-esteem issues of what I thought and felt about myself, but I also needed to work on changing the old codependent behavior that I had been using for years.

I started watching myself very closely to see how these two themes tied together. Years of meditation (being aware of my own mind) and years as a counselor (being attuned to the minds of others) gave me the skills to pick up the patterns quickly. What I noticed was that each time I didn't feel happy, I could track my feelings to something negative that I was telling myself. But more often, rather than to notice that internal criticism, I would habitually and automatically undertake some compulsive behavior to "fill the void," to make me feel better.

At the time I was, coincidentally, experimenting with certain dietary changes, and I had eliminated the foods I normally used to cover my feelings--chocolate, cookies, crackers and coffee. What I observed was that if one compulsive behavior wasn't an option, I would easily switch to another--anything to take my mind off the emotional discomfort. If chocolate was out, keeping busy would help; if sugar was out, sex would serve. Cigarettes, alcohol, a shopping spree, watching TV, burying myself in my work, biting my nails--I noticed it was fairly easy to substitute one for the other, as long as it helped me to avoid negative feelings about myself.

Soon it became evident to me that the codependent behaviors were not exclusive to relationships; that one could actually have a codependent relationship with almost anything or anyone that promised to provide a sense of value and fill the emptiness, however temporarily. It might be another person, a career, a one-night-stand, a volunteer job, a chocolate binge, a bottle of tequila, a trip to Macy's, or a weekend in front of the television set. I broadened my view of *codependency* and began to see it as the *adaptive behavior patterns whereby one achieves the illusion of self-esteem by using an external source to achieve temporary beliefs of self-worth and feelings of happiness.*

For many people the preferred codependent behaviors are so habitual that we call them compulsive or addictive, implying we have no control over them. Codependence generally refers to mutually dependent behaviors within a relationship with another person, in particular a spouse or lover, although it often exists between parent and child, co-workers, friends, and other human relationships.

But, as previously mentioned, we can actually have a "codependent" relationship with food, work, alcohol, drugs, gambling, and any other compulsive or addictive behavior or substance that we use to make ourselves feel better. In *Codependence: Misunderstood, Mistreated*, Anne Schaef (1986) presents a similar concept, calling it "the addictive process" and a "disease that has many forms and expressions" (p. 21). What makes our behavior *co*-dependent is that we, in effect, create a trade agreement with the other person (or habit). This agreement says, "I will give you power over me if you will make me feel good." Then, when we have negative thoughts and feelings about ourselves, it becomes an immediate stimulus for the automatic codependent behavior of our preference.

What becomes evident is that the real issue is not codependency but self-esteem. The codependent behavior becomes the clue that low self-esteem is occurring internally. Codependency, in other words, is the symptom. Its cause is twofold, as the stories above illustrate. The core and primary cause is the lack of *self-esteem*, the negative beliefs and feelings about not being good enough. Yet there is a secondary, equally powerful cause of codependent behavior, and that is *habit*. When we are growing up within a dysfuntional family (and all families have some degree of dysfunction), we adopt certain codependent behaviors in order to adapt and survive. In time these patterns become a regular part of our repertoire, and they stay with us through habit long after they serve a function, unless we consciously undertake to change them.

GETTING STARTED ON CHANGE

When we get tired enough of the old habits and patterns that keep creating pain in our lives, we start looking for ways to change. We all have the capacity to live our lives in the ways we've always dreamed. But it takes the decision to make changes, the courage to examine our own patterns, and the determination to practice doing things in a different way.

The tools and techniques in the book *work*; for me they are almost magic--*when* I use them. A friend once said that the spiritual path, or the path of growth, is a slow process of chip, chip, chipping away. Our sculpture is not complete until the day we die. The person who has given up learning, growing, and working on himself, has given up his purpose for life. Do the exercises and learn the processes taught in this book.

Make them a part of how you see and live your life. You will experience life as a constant unfolding, always interesting, always exciting, and always expanding.

EXERCISES

1.   Go out and get a notebook right now if you do not already have one. A full-sized spiral notebook is the best. Use it to do the excercises in this book, and also to make any notes, or just to "unload" when you feel like it. You might call it your "Healing Journal."

2.   Make a list of the areas in which you experience low self-esteem. Use very specific examples, such as "When I don't complete work by the deadline I set for myself," or "When other women look better than I do," or "When Sharon comes home late." Consider your relationships, career, family life, love life, finances, spiritual life, intellect, health, appearance, and emotions. The list might be a page or two long.

3.   Make two columns. On the right side, make a list of the things you *most* want other people to know about you. Then list the things you *least* want others to know about you. Next, on the left side of each list, note what your reason is for wanting someone to know or not know these things. What do you notice about how other's opinions affect your self-esteem?

2

Thoughts Create Our Reality

STARTING WITH THE MIND

Thoughts create our reality. Thoughts are very real and tangible. They are the origin and reason for everything we create and experience in our lives. We do not do or perceive anything that does not exist initially as a thought. No war has ever been fought, no peace has ever been won, that did not occur in the minds of the people first. People who are wealthy think it's all right to have money. People who are poor think they'll never be rich.

Once I had a car with an engine that seemed to be in poor condition. I decided perhaps if the car were totalled I'd have a better chance of getting my money's worth from the thing. In the next week I had three near collisions. In the last one, a person turned and headed directly towards me going the wrong direction in my lane. We screeched to a halt, our bumpers barely touching as we both finally stopped. That caught my attention. I realized I had best change my thoughts or I could end up totalled as well. I decided I could get my money's worth a different way, and I did; the car served me well for several more years before I sold it to someone whose hobby was car repair.

When we believe something, we act as if it is true, whether it is or not. An obvious example is the anorexic who tells herself she is fat, and only sees a fat person in the mirror. Someone who says, "I can't talk to my family" will believe that statement and never even try new approaches to communication. People who say to themselves, "I have to lose weight before I can ever have a man (or woman)," believe this statement and do nothing to create social interaction, despite the fact that most overweight people are in relationships with the opposite sex. A very dramatic example of the power of thought is in the case of people with multiple personalities. One personality may require glasses while another doesn't, one will have abilities another doesn't have, and one may have an illness which the other personalities in the same body do not have.

What becomes incredibly evident, once we are aware of the powerful effect of our thoughts, is that the things we say to ourselves *become* our reality. We live our lives according to what we tell ourselves. Aaron Beck (1979) explains that when we incorrectly think we are being rejected, we will react with the same negative feelings that occur if we were actually being rejected. A person who says, "I'll never have the kind of job I want," either acts depressed and shows up late for an interview, or simply never even looks for the ideal job. A person whose mind says "I am ugly," will tend to have poor hygiene and dress in a shabby manner, eliminating the possiblity that anyone might ever think otherwise. In subtle but powerful ways we communicate our thoughts to others and gather as much evidence as possible from our environment to confirm those thoughts.

All of us have a constant monologue running inside of our minds. Although most of them are subconscious, we have hundreds of thoughts each minute. Sometimes we have conflicting thoughts within us and we run a dialogue; at times there may seem to be a whole room full of people discussing and arguing inside our heads. As we go through the activities of a normal day, our minds are constantly thinking: planning, organizing, deciphering, interpreting, remembering, contemplating, pondering, figuring, categorizing, analyzing, judging, worrying, daydreaming, imagining, and carrying on the many other mental functions that distinguish us as human beings. In *What To Say When You Talk to Yourself*, Shad Helmstetter (1986) says that we are thinking machines which never shut down.

These thoughts, or internal conversations, have been given many names, such as "mindtalk," "self-talk," "brain-chatter," "self-statements," "self-verbalizations," and "internal dialogue." I use the term "mindtalk" because I think it best describes the phenomenon. It addresses thoughts about the self as well as others, and it includes either a single train of thoughts or conversation between our different parts. I learned this term from Brad Brown and Roy Whitten, founders of The Life Training seminars. They have a wonderful way of presenting transformational material in a manner that is both experiential and meaningful on a conceptual level.

In many situations our mindtalk helps us. It is how we arrange our perceptions and organize our lives. But when mindtalk is critical and judgmental, it becomes the source of negative feelings about ourselves and others. And when it is habitually negative towards ourselves, it becomes the source of low self-esteem. *It is this negative mindtalk toward ourselves that we must examine and change if we are to convert low self-esteem and codependent behavior into high self-esteem.*

HOW MINDTALK WORKS

Mindtalk may include a single thought, a train of thoughts, or a belief. Thoughts pass through the mind in a split second. We have so many of them in one minute, that it is impossible to be consciously aware of more than a few of them. When a given thought is repeated many times, and when we have begun to perceive it as "the truth," we call it a belief. Once we have a particular belief, we tend to continue to think in the same way. We do this because the brain attempts to tie any new information that it receives to something that is already in our mind (Helmstetter, 1986).

Beliefs are like "resident thoughts;" we may not consciously think them, but they are part of our mental "computer program." Once we believe certain mindtalk, or think that it is true, we will do all we can to keep away evidence to the contrary. It becomes a regular part of how we see ourselves and our world, integrated, often on a subconscious level, into our belief system. Years of growing up in the same environment reinforces the same beliefs over and over. When we get older, these beliefs have become comfortable and familiar; our lives have been organized around them for a long time and we are reluctant to give them up.

Some years ago I bought a wonderful new dress. But my mindtalk was, "If you look too nice around other women, they won't like you." A friend walked by, stopped dead in her tracks and exclaimed, "Oo-o, what a beautiful dress! Is it new?" My response was, "Oh, this is just an old rag." I wasn't willing to allow the compliment into my awareness. It didn't fit my belief system. Today when I receive a compliment, I get a great big smile on my face and say, "Well, thanks!" I now believe that I not only deserve nice things, but I deserve nice compliments as well.

Wendy, a former client, had the belief that she was not lovable. Although she was in a relationship with Ben, a very loving man, she ignored--simply did not perceive--his loving gestures. She was constantly fearful when he was not being particularly attentive. What she allowed into her conscious mind was only those experiences which confirmed her mindtalk. By shutting out the love she received and focusing on only the negative, she continued to confirm her mindtalk that she was not lovable. It was not until Ben threatened to leave, frustrated by the constant rejection of his love, that Wendy sought help in changing some of the habitual mindtalk by which she was keeping him at a distance. Our reality is absolutely created by the thoughts we have. When we believe the mindtalk, our behavior perpetuates and confirms those thoughts.

If we believe that women are always manipulative, or men are always children, that is the only type of person we will ever see. We will be blind to direct and honest women and to mature and responsible men. They simply will not exist for us; they will be invisible. Unfortunately, so often we are not even aware that we have such thoughts. Yet, we will be drawn like a magnet to those people who confirm our familiar beliefs, even those which are not conscious. It is no wonder that the child of an alcoholic will marry one alcoholic after another or that an abused child will marry an abusing spouse. It is only by changing both our beliefs about others and by allowing ourselves the belief that we are worthy of good in our lives, that we can create the kind of reality for ourselves that brings happiness.

I was at one time a therapist for an overweight clinic. It was a medically-supervised, nutritionally-supplemented fasting program in which clients were allowed to fast up to a year. What I found was that people would get down to a certain weight, and no amount of fasting would bring their weight lower until they resolved the issues that kept them overweight. For some the belief was, "I have to be big and strong so I don't get hurt." For others it was "If I let myself be too attractive, I'll have to deal with sex." There were even others whose mindtalk ran, "If I let myself be too attractive, my husband (wife) will be jealous, so I have to stay ugly." How amazingly potent these beliefs are! Once these often subconscious beliefs were uncovered and changed, the weight would typically continue to drop away.

One of the more interesting phenomena that dramatically demonstrates the manner in which we actually embody our mindtalk is evidenced in certain therapeutic bodywork that is currently being practiced. In deep tissue massage such as Rolfing, in body-centered psychotherapies such as Hakomi and Bioenergetics, as well as in Educational and Psychological Kinesiology, it has been demonstrated that deep emotions and the accompanying beliefs are often "stored" in the body when they have not been fully experienced or expressed. That is to say, we "stuff" our feelings or keep them at a subconscious level by creating tension in our bodies to hold those feelings inside.

Tightness in the chest or heart area, for example, usually brings up issues about being loved. Tension in the shoulders and upper back often have to do with mindtalk which says, "I do not have enough support," or "I have to support others beyond my capacity."

Tightness in the throat and neck are often related to beliefs about not being able to express oneself. Louise Hay (1984) has a wonderful book called *You Can Heal Your Life*, in which she details many of the physical manifestations of certain thought processes.

It is not a part of our traditional educational system at this time to learn about the mind, how it works, the nature of thoughts or mindtalk, or the effects of belief systems created by mindtalk. Heretofore that has been an area of study reserved primarily for psychologists (and, in some cultures, for spiritual leaders). Yet our minds are the creative forces of our lives. We each have the right, or perhaps we should say the responsibility, to know better what goes on inside of us and how to use it in a way that does not sabotage us, but rather supports and expands our lives.

THE MIND: GETTING TO KNOW IT

Obviously, the mind is an important instrument that we *need* for our livelihood. It is a vital and exciting part of our humanity. For the purposes of this book, when we refer to the mind, to beliefs, and to mindtalk, we are generally addressing the ways in which the mind creates low self-esteem. Yet the mind has many functions, one of which is evaluation and discernment. Mindtalk is not always negative. It is the means by which we make wise decisions and choices for our lives. However, when the mindtalk is by habit judgmental and critical of ourselves and others, when it ceases to play a constructive role because of old negative patterns, we need to examine those beliefs and notice that they no longer play the protective role in our lives that they may have played when we were young. Then we can change the old patterns into new ones that empower us and bring us joy.

One of the most effective ways of developing this skill is through meditation, whether we call it stress management, biofeedback, TM, or contemplation. I find that clients who regularly take time to be alone with themselves experience a much faster and easier growth process. They are more able to be aware of their own feelings, their mindtalk, and in particular, their subconscious thoughts. Daily meditation is also recommended as part of every 12-Step Program. Meditation, or a quiet private time, not only allows greater accessibility to our own thoughts, but also teaches us the control needed to change habitual thoughts when we see those thoughts are not serving us.

Another means to becoming familiar with our conscious and subconscious thoughts involves allowing ourselves to be in touch with our own feelings. In Chapter Three, we will explore in depth a procedure I call the Reprogramming Process, which is profoundly helpful in getting to know ourselves. There are many paths to improving our lives, limited only by our own level of dedication to our growth. But, if we truly seek, we do, indeed, find the way that is best for each of us.

In the Eastern tradition there is the story of a man who is walking down the road and gets a thorn stuck in his foot. He jumps around in pain, doing nothing to remove the thorn, and in fact, makes the pain worse with all of his writhing and complaining. Finally, he decides to sit quietly and comtemplate the situation. Almost immediately he realizes that he can use another thorn to remove the first. So it is with the mind. It is the mind that thinks the negative and critical thoughts; it is also the mind that can replace them with honest self-acknowledgment and self-acceptance. Thus we can use the mind to improve the quality of what the mind creates.

The habitual negative thoughts about ourselves, and the projections that we are unlovable and unworthy, are NOT the truth. In fact, they are lies, erroneous mind-talk we have told to ourselves. Sometimes those thoughts look and feel true because we have gathered so much evidence to prove them over the years. But if we believe that we are made in God's image, which is stated not only in the *Bible* but in the texts of many other religions, then we know our essential nature is divine. It is up to *us* to cease focusing on our human frailties, except in a constructive way, and to honor that within us which is unique and wonderful and very special.

HOW THE THOUGHTS GOT THERE

We *learned* to be who we are when we were very small. That is to say, we learned how to perceive and how to react to our world. Even when we were pre-verbal, we started to form concepts of ourselves and the world. By the time we were two we already had very solid beliefs about whether or not the world was a nurturing place, whether or not we were lovable, and what rules we had to follow to get our needs met. With each event in our lives we responded with thoughts that evaluated that event and taught us how to best respond to the outside world. Positive experiences resulted in thoughts about our mastery, skill, and self-worth. Negative experiences resulted in thoughts, or mindtalk, about being more careful, about what we had to do to avoid future pain, and sometimes about low self-worth. Soon, with repeated reinforcement, this mindtalk became a part of our belief system.

Aaron Beck (1979) explains that our early experiences provide the basis for forming negative concepts about ourselves, the future, and the world around us. These negative perspectives may have been formed in relation to those early events, but they are often reactivated by circumstances which are similar to those initial experiences. Thus we repeat through the years the negative *interpretations* of events that we learned when we were very young.

A person who is skilled at healthy parenting will separate the issues of appropriate behavior from issues of self-worth. Children can be corrected or even punished while simultaneously being reassured that they are inherently loved and valuable. For example, rather than, "You stupid brat, go to your room and don't come out!" we might say, "Joey, I love you, but that behavior is not OK. Go sit in your room for ten minutes." Another example might be, "Nancy, I've had a bad day and I'm feeling grouchy. I usually enjoy being with you, but right now I need to be alone. Please play somewhere else while I'm trying to cook."

Yet when parents are stressed, out of balance, and struggling with their own self-esteem issues, it is not unusual for them to vent their frustrations on their children, or at minimum, forget to be psychologically attuned to their kids. In some families there is not so much the style of venting frustrations but of cool withholding of love or subtle manipulation in order to elicit the preferred behavior from the children. Whatever the family's particular patterns and style are, a child will develop from a very early age a set of beliefs about himself, the world outside of himself, and what should be done or felt in order to get along.

There is often an entire mass of beliefs that is stimulated when even a single unpleasant event occurs. I remember standing at the kitchen counter with the top of the counter well above my head, so I must have been about five years old. I wanted to play with the round cake tins, the ones with removable bottoms. My mother was busy at the other end of the kitchen, but from the essentially egocentric perspective of a small child, I was only concerned with the cake tins, and I persisted in whining about them until I got my mother's attention. But when I got it, she was already exasperated with being interrupted. "Want, want, want, you always want," she yelled, and I was immediately whisked off my feet and shut in my room. I cried for what seemed like hours. Extrapolating from that event, my mindtalk very quietly in the back of my mind said, "I always want too much; I should never want; I'm a big bother to my mother; I take up too much of her time; I shouldn't want anything; when I want things it makes people angry; I don't deserve things I want; I shouldn't have fun; I shouldn't want pretty things; I'm a selfish person; I'm no good; and, my parents don't want me."

If this barrage of mindtalk seems unrealistic and excessive, keep in mind that most of it occurs on a subconscious level. Most of us would not want to admit that we think such things. However, it is events such as these, and repetition of similar situations over the some sixteen to twenty years of early life, that set the beliefs in place and reinforced them. We not only tend to think the same kinds of thoughts that our parents habitually thought (Hay, 1984), but we add to that our own set of interpretations of what is occurring to us and around us.

Yet, it is important to understand that we ourselves perceived the situations and gave them meaning. In other words, it is *our own minds* that are responsible for how we see ourselves and our world. My mindtalk might have been, "My mother is having a bad day today, I'd better go play in my room." But instead, I decided that I wasn't OK. And thus, a belief about what I deserved and what I was worth became a part of my perceptions that stayed the same for many years.

SETTING OUR WORLD STRAIGHT

It would be nice if our parents--and the other people around us when we were growing up--were perfect. But they were not, just as we are not. By now it is probably obvious that we are not going to change our parents--or our spouse, or anyone else. How much we have already tried! And even if we could, it is not going to change how we feel. *The only thing we can do to change and to heal our self-worth is to change what's in our minds,* in our own selves. It is important to understand that even though those thoughts may have become a part of our reality when we were small, and even though childhood circumstances helped to create the low self-esteem, still, we are the only ones who can change them now. We are the only ones who can change our own mindtalk from "I'm selfish and I shouldn't want" to a belief that says, "I do deserve to have nice things, and I am often very unselfish and giving."

Yet, it is often frightening to look at changing ourselves. When we don't like things the way they are, the first thing we try to do is change what is external to us. How many times have we thought we could be happy if people would just be the way we wanted them to be? If the boss were more appreciative, if our spouse were a little more loving, the children more disciplined, if our parents had been more patient, then we could be happy--right? Sometimes it seems as if everything around us conspires to make things hard. Why is it that people aren't just a little more cooperative?

We seem to have a natural and very human ten-dency to wish that circumstances and people would change to make our lives easier and better. When problems arise, we tend to look outside of ourselves for the source of change. We try to get others to see things our way. We feel angry or hurt when loved ones are different from how we want them to be. Whether we blame, manipulate, pout, feign detachment or sweet-talk, we all have our favorite way of getting others to change.

Our culture supports the notion that changing what's outside of us will make us happy; in fact, it is the cornerstone of our economic system. We are bombarded with messages that say, "If you feel pain, take a pill. If you feel ugly, buy something to make you beautiful. If you are bored, watch TV. If you feel empty, eat or drink. If you feel lonely, get a divorce (or get married if you're already divorced)." These messages are all around us: if you manipulate people and your environment properly, you can be satisfied and feel good about yourself.

Obviously, however, there is something amiss here. Sooner or later we notice that trying to force things to change doesn't work. Changing what is external to us is often simply a temporary "fix." It becomes painfully clear that these manipulations are nothing but stop-gap measures. Does the threat of a month with no dessert deter the little one from squeezing the toothpaste in the middle for any longer than a day? Does a new dress make us feel better about ourselves for any longer than an hour, or maybe slightly longer? We can still be bored after ten hours of TV, still feel lonely after three marriages, and still feel empty after a six-course meal or six margaritas.

What becomes very evident is that any efforts to change our feelings about ourselves by attempting to force other people or outside events to be different is futile. The power to change things lies within, but there is only one area over which we have domain, and that is ourselves. As much as we may want other people and outside events to adjust for our comfort, the truth is: *the only thing we can do to make ourselves feel better is to change the way we interpret or perceive things and the way we act*. We may not like it, but it's a fact.

E, I, AND F

Learning to change ourselves is no easy task. It takes the courage to look inside, the willingness to be vulnerable and to make mistakes, and the determination to keep chipping away at the old beliefs and habit patterns. This is much easier if we understand the dynamics by which our minds operate.

Our lives are filled with many *events* to which we have negative reactions. The boss complains, the spouse is grouchy, the kids fight. Some events are traumatic and life-altering. Others are minor irritations we barely notice. When an event occurs, we generally experience a *feeling*, an emotional reaction. (In psychological terms we would say that a "stimulus" is followed by a "response.") We tend to believe that the event is the *cause* of that feeling. If that were true, it might be written,

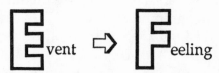

When our spouse comes home late without calling (event), our first inclination is often to blame the other person for "hurting me" (feeling). Suppose there is an event where a friend comments, "Boy, that was

dumb." When we react with hurt, we think that our feeling or emotion was caused by the other's statement. When we get depressed after being bypassed for a promotion, we think that it was the event of not being promoted that caused our feelings. In the way we use our language, we say "You made me feel bad." "You made me angry," "She makes me happy," "That makes me sick." We think that the event causes our emotional responses.

However, in actuality it is *not the event, but our interpretation of the event that creates the pain.* The interpretation is the specific mindtalk and the underlying beliefs we have about that event. For example, one person who hears, "You sure are silly," interprets it to mean that he is very clever, and feels proud. Another hears the same statement, interprets it to mean he is foolish, and feels shame. One person who hears, "Oh, she's a housewife and a mother" may think of that as a laudable occupation, interpret it as a compliment, and feel pleased; another may not value that profession, interpret the statement as a criticism, and feel embarrassed.

Because thoughts flash through our minds at such an incredibly rapid speed, and because we interpret events in ways that have been habitual for years, we do not particularly notice the mindtalk that has intervened between the event and our emotional response. The event *appears* to cause the feelings, but in actuality, it is our interpretation of the event that stimulates our feelings. Our formula, then, is more accurately written,

$$\boxed{\textsf{E}}\text{vent} \Rightarrow \boxed{\textsf{I}}\text{nterpretation} \Rightarrow \boxed{\textsf{F}}\text{eeling}$$

or, *the event stimulates the interpretation which causes the feeling.*

Understanding this basic concept is crucial to healing old codependent habits and creating strong self-esteem. This concept was introduced by Albert Ellis who observed that emotional disturbances do not stem from the events that precede them, but from the mind's interpretation of those events. Unfortunately, when we think the outside events are the cause of our negative feelings, we then believe that we cannot change them. Rather, according to Ellis (1975), we make ourselves happy or miserable by our perceptions, attitudes, and what we say to ourselves *about* those outside events. In other words, it is the incorrect processing of information by our minds, not the event itself, which results in our experience of pain (Beck, Rush, Shaw, Emery 1979).

When we become aware of what our mind says in response to any given event, *we can choose whether we will use the old interpretation or begin living with a new, more supportive and self-loving view of the event.* It is the mind's interpretation, or the mindtalk about that event, that is different in each situation. Our minds respond in ways that are unique to each of us; different from anyone else's mind. We cannot change what other people do and say, but we can change the way we perceive what happens in our world.

When we change our interpretation--our mindtalk--about any given event, it changes our feelings, which in turn changes our actions. For example, suppose we hear someone call, "Hey, Gorgeous." If we interpret this with mindtalk that says "That low-classed slob is not treating me with respect," then we may feel anger, turn our nose up, and stomp away. On the other hand, if our interpretation is mindtalk that says "Thirty-six years old and he still thinks I look good--

good for me!" we might feel delighted and flash that other person a big smile. In other words, our interpretation not only affects how we feel, but it ultimately results in our choice of actions. And those actions in turn affect how others respond to us. Ultimately it creates a feedback system in which it sooner or later becomes evident that we create our own reality.

The following was part of a dialogue with a student in one of my Self-Esteem workshops. It demonstrates an exciting shift that she experienced when she realized the effect that some of her mindtalk had had on her life:

Betty: I came from an abusive family. My father was abusive to me, and he was also abused. As I have been working on this issue, I have realized that my ex-husband was an alcoholic, most of the men in my life--bosses and other relationships--have all been alcoholic or abusive, or have come from alcoholic or abusive families. So my mindtalk about men has always been that they are abusive. And I have a feeling that my weight ties into this.

CB: No doubt your choice of men and your weight are tied together. Let's see. How does your mindtalk say you have to react to men?

Betty: I have to...(pauses, then laughs) *keep them away from me! I have to be big and strong and not vulnerable!* This is the first time I've been able to see the whole picture, the repetition of the patterns I have lived a long time believing this was true--and it isn't.

What Betty discovered from this short exchange was that she had kept herself constantly overweight because her mindtalk had said that this was the only way to protect herself from abuse. By recognizing the fallacy in this thought habit, she could now find other, more healthy ways of experiencing her power without being abusive to her own body.

HOW WE CREATED LOW SELF-ESTEEM

As we go through the process of learning to be aware of and examine our mindtalk, it is sometimes surprising to see the kinds of things we say to and about ourselves. They are often things we would *never* say to a friend. In fact, we would rarely be so rude as to say them to someone we disliked. But we tend to be merciless with ourselves, and thus, without realizing it, create low self-esteem.

A client recently called up her boyfriend, excited to talk with him. "Hi, this is Kathy!", she said. "Who?" came his answer (event). Immediately she felt crushed, anxious, and devastated (feeling). When she stopped to examine her interpretation, she discovered that her mindtalk ran, "He wants to hurt me; he doesn't care about me any more, he's met someone else and wants to get rid of me; I'm ugly; I'm stupid; I'm a fool for thinking he'd care about me; I'm not good enough; there's no reason for me to be alive." All of this raced through her mind in a split second. Her *interpretation* of that event was that her boyfriend was rejecting her, and she compounded her discomfort by berating herself with criticisms and judgments. She later found out that he had fumbled the phone when he picked it up and had simply not heard her.

If we take the E-I-F model one step further, we get another clue to low self-esteem. What often happens is that either our mindtalk or our feelings can in themselves become another event. We may interpret the original event with negative mindtalk, but in addition usually *also* interpret both our mindtalk and the resulting feelings with *further* negative mindtalk and feelings. Thus we may react to an event, but also react to our reaction. For example, we may feel angry about a situation, but then tell ourselves that we "shouldn't feel angry" and then feel ashamed. According to Satir (1983), low self-esteem results from what we communicate to ourselves about our feelings and the attempt to conceal rather than acknowledge their existence.

Our negative interpretations about our interpretations and feelings, and our negative feelings about our feelings and interpretations are at the root of low self-esteem. These deeper and deeper levels of mindtalk and emotional reaction lead to the downward spiral that is sometimes associated with depression and feelings of defeat. So, using the above example, the event--"Who?"--resulted in Kathy's mindtalk that her boyfriend wanted to hurt her. Her emotional reaction was pain. But the *thought* that he wanted to hurt her became *another event* which brought up further mindtalk--that he didn't want her and had met someone else--and her reaction was anxiety. This then became still another event, to which her mindtalk said she was ugly, a fool, and not good enough. At this point she experienced the emotion of desperation. Thus, sometimes our mindtalk will feed on itself, creating a series of events, interpretations, and feelings, looking something like the diagram on the opposite page.

When such a chain reaction occurs, when we level one criticism after another at ourselves, we experience the kind of dejection or depression from which it is difficult to extract ourselves. We have stacked so many layers of negative thoughts and judgments upon ourselves that it is hard to find our way out. Once we make such statements to ourselves, we then tend not only to see those statements as the truth, but

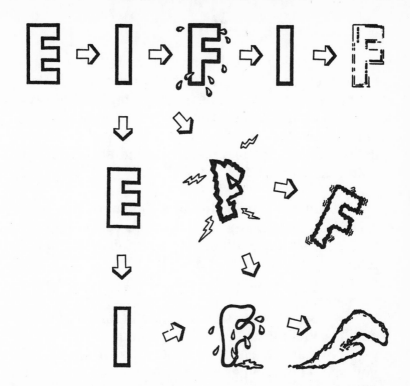

we also tend to see them as categorical, absolute, and unchangeable. We cease to examine the validity of these statements and make them a permanent part of our reality.

We assumed many of our beliefs when we were two, three and four years old. But they can wreak havoc in our lives when we are twenty or thirty, or until we die, unless we stop the process of telling ourselves negative things that are essentially untrue and begin to acknowledge our own special and wonderful qualities. We can do this simply by taking charge of our lives and deciding that it is time to treat ourselves in a loving way. *Our thoughts create our reality, and it is time to create our lives in a way that makes us feel good about ourselves!*

EXERCISES

1.   Make three columns. On the left side write a few sentences about five or ten different incidents to which you reacted with negative feelings. Then, in the middle column, write your interpretation of those situations, in other words, the mindtalk you had about them. Make particular note of mindtalk relating to your self-worth.

2.   In the third column, write some new interpretations for each event that are based on the belief that you are unconditionally acceptable and worthwhile. Notice if you feel different about any of those events by interpreting them in a different manner.

3.   Set a goal to sit alone quietly for a while each day. Decide if it will be for five minutes, twenty, thirty, or whatever. Use that time to be in touch with yourself, your feelings, your thoughts and your body, with no external distractions. Whether it be for formal meditation, or just a private quiet time, give yourself permission to do this every day.

3

Getting To Know
Ourselves

STALKING THE SUBCONSIOUS MINDTALK

In order to become better aware of the subconsious mindtalk which has created low self-esteem and codependent patterns--and to do something about it--it is necessary to find a way to access these thoughts. To do this we must bypass the conscious mind so that we can get in touch with the subtle inner messages that run our lives.

The conscious mind is a sly one. It doesn't want to admit some of the deepest fears and judgments that we have about ourselves. Its job, rather, is to keep us functioning, to take care of our everyday lives. Therefore the conscious mind will often do its best to cover up or "stuff" our feelings and critical mindtalk. It does this by various "devious" means, such as rationalization, denial, and blaming others. Yet it is important to realize that we do not mean to be dishonest; we do this "cover-up" unconsciously in order to protect ourselves from pain. And we are not alone in this; it is a normal human trait. So, to get to the root of the thoughts that have sabotaged our self-esteem, we need to somehow bypass that protective surface layer and discover those troublesome subconscious thoughts that are creating havoc in our lives.

For decades any form of psychotherapy was a very slow process. People could spend years in therapy analyzing all the things their parents did "wrong" and yet never feel substantially better. Sometimes it was forgotten that their parents had parents, who also had parents. The *Bible* is quite accurate when it says that the sins of the parents will be visited on their children for many generations. Fortunately, psychology has grown up over the years, and we now know that no matter what our ancestors did, we can begin to reverse the dysfunctional patterns by taking the responsibility for change in our own lives.

When we decide to do what it takes to improve the quality of our lives, we are taking the courageous step to stop putting our energy into trying to make others be different. *We can choose instead, to start gently peeling away our own protective layers so we can be in touch with the thoughts and beliefs that limit us from being all that we can be.* We are saying, in effect, "The buck stops here; I choose to take responsibility to heal my life, no matter what went on before."

As we have demonstrated, the creative force--that which creates joy or sorrow--is our thoughts. There are many kinds of thoughts, and we have touched on several of them. In order to better understand how our minds work, it is useful to further define some of our terms. The broadest term we are using is "thoughts," which covers all the cognitive functions of the mind. "Mindtalk" specifically refers to a series of thoughts which make up our internal conversation, whether we are conscious of it or not. "Beliefs" are thoughts that we have decided are true, whether they are true or not. Whereas mindtalk is the specific thoughts we may have at any given time, beliefs are core thoughts, the programing from which other thoughts arise. Our "interpretation" of any given event is the conceptual framework by which we perceive the event. It is the way we organize our experience (Del Prince, 1989). Our *interpretations are based on our beliefs, and are expressed by our mindtalk.*

An important type of thought which tends to have a negative effect on our self-esteem is our "judgments." Judgments are our beliefs about what is right and what is wrong. Having a set of values is important for each of us, even though no two people agree exactly as to what those values are. It is when the judgments become the basis for rejecting ourselves that they become a problem. For many of us growing up in a dysfunctional family, we learned that always being happy, trying not to feel anger or hurt, and putting others' needs before our own was "good." Expressing our opinions, attitudes, needs and feelings was "bad." Thus we learned to judge ourselves as good or bad, right or wrong, valuable or valueless, based on the feedback we got from the people around us. By thus learning to judge ourselves, we developed the habit of interpreting many of the events in our lives as indications that we were bad or that we did not have value as a person.

Such judgments fall into two categories. One is the perfectionistic *demands* we place on ourselves to live up to the expectations of others and ourselves in order that we may be accepted. This kind of judgment is usually phrased in mindtalk that starts with "I should," "I have to," "I shouldn't," etc. The second type of judgment is the *criticisms* we level at ourselves when we do not live up to the unrealistic demands we place on ourselves. Criticisms are usually mindtalk which is phrased as specific insults, such as "I'm stupid," "I'm a pig," "I'm too emotional," or "I can't do anything right." While criticism can be of a constructive nature, we often use it to devalue ourselves, thus leading to low self-esteem.

In addition to thoughts, the other important element in understanding ourselves is our "feelings," or "emotions." These terms are used somewhat interchangeably, although "feeling" also applies to the physical reaction that accompanies the emotion. For each emotion that we experience there is a biochemical reaction within the body. Learning to be aware of the physical aspect of our feelings as well as the emotional component is an important part of gathering data as we get to know ourselves.

FEELING OUR FEELINGS--
THE DOOR OUT OF PAIN

Allowing ourselves to experience our feelings is the key to healing ourselves. Whether we realize it or not, we have all at some time put a great deal of energy into avoiding our feelings--our emotions as well as our physical feelings. We have denied our feelings for various reasons--we have been afraid of them, ashamed of them, or we have thought of our feelings as bad or abnormal (Wegscheider-Cruse, 1987).

For many of us, avoiding our feelings was the "self-control" we were taught as children. Others have discovered suppressing emotions to be socially expedient. Still others learned to "stuff" or "shut down" feelings because they were simply too painful. Sometimes we ourselves are not even aware that the feelings are there, although others may read them in our facial expression, body language, and tone of voice.

Often we will avoid feelings by filling our time, space or bodies with codependency and other addictive and compulsive behaviors and substances. Or, we may hide our feelings from ourselves and other people by acting superior, joking, or by tightening our muscles and holding the feelings in the physical body rather than experiencing them emotionally. Another way we stuff our feelings is by covering a deeper feeling with one that is easier to handle, such as expressing hurt when we don't want to be in touch with our anger.

When the oil light comes on in the dashboard of our car, we do not take a hammer and smash the light. We open the hood, check to see what is needed, and give our car the attention it requires so it will run properly. When we attempt to suppress or avoid our feelings--covering them over with some form of codependent or addictive behavior or substance--it is like breaking the light that says we need to add oil. The pain gives us information; it lets us know we need to open our hoods, so to speak. We need to look inside and see what adjustments will help us run better. *In order to heal ourselves it is necessary that we give honor to and allow expression of our feelings, so that we can look inside our minds and adjust the belief systems that are causing the pain.*

If we are experiencing unpleasant feelings, it is an indicator that we are thinking something negative and believing it is true (Burns, 1980). When we allow ourselves to experience those feelings, the subconscious mindtalk comes to the surface (Brown and Whitten, 1983). Thus, as we tune in to our feelings, we open the flow of mindtalk, much of which is suppressed by the various compulsive and codependent behaviors we use to avoid our feelings.

If we have grown up with the belief that our feelings are not acceptable, it may be difficult at first to even know what our feelings are. Nick, a client who started therapy shortly after his wife had left him, was very aware of his wife's anger and resentment, but drew a complete blank each time I asked him how he felt. He began carrying a list of feelings with him to our sessions, and referred to it often. Thus he took the initiative to learn about himself in this creative way. As Beattie (1987) explains, we are often very aware of what others are feeling, why they feel that way, and what they will probably do because of that feeling. Yet we do not know what *we* are feeling, nor what to do about it. Many of us have no concept of taking responsibility for our own emotional selves.

Being honest with ourselves about what is going on inside of us, and giving ourselves permission to fully experience our genuine feelings, are therefore the essential ingredients to any successful internal work. These are steps we cannot bypass in claiming our self-esteem. As soon as an uncomfortable or unpleasant event is experienced, the feelings immediately come to the surface. Our automatic reaction is often to attempt to suppress the feelings rather than to pay attention to them and allow ourselves to feel them. Emotions we typically try to bury are hurt, anger, resentment, pain, jealousy, guilt, shame, depression, anxiety, frustration, loneliness, numbness, shock and embarrassment. These are but a few of an enormous range of possible emotions. Love, joy, delight and compassion are also feelings, although they are rarely experienced at times when we have low self-esteem.

Emotions can be felt within the body. The stomach may tighten, the jaw may stiffen, or there may be pain in the heart area or tension in the neck; the shoulders may hunch or sag. Sometimes the physical feeling is our first clue that we are experiencing an emotional reaction. For example, anger often results in tension in the stomach and intestinal area or tightness in the jaw. Hurt and loneliness are often felt in the heart. Embarrassment is sometimes expressed by the body when blood comes to the surface of the skin and there is an experience of heat in the face and neck. The fear of expressing oneself can manifest as tightness in the throat. Shame may be expressed as a drooping of the shoulders. A feeling of shock may result in the experience of numbness all over the body.

In order to love and accept ourselves unconditionally, we need to learn to know and accept ourselves as we are. To do this, we must release the idea that any of our feelings are unacceptable, allowing ourselves to fully attend to and feel them. In *Why Am I Afraid to Tell You Who I Am*, John Powell (1969) explains that emotions are not inherently good or bad; they simply exist. In learning to know ourselves and in communicating with others, we need to recognize, experience, and accept our feelings. Then we can choose appropriate ways of expressing them and/or sharing them with others.

To help ourselves be more fully in touch with our feelings, we can allow the body to help us. We can do this by exaggerating the posture we fall into when we experience our emotions. We may notice tightness in the chest or stomach, and put our hands over that part of the body in order to magnify our awareness of the feeling there (Del Prince, 1989). We may notice ourselves holding our breath when we focus on an event to which we have reacted. This is another way to stuff our feelings. To counter this natural reaction, we can *inhale deeply*, allow our lips to be slightly parted, and as we exhale, allow the sound to come out of the mouth which expresses that feeling. For example, if we feel angry there may be a growling sound; if we feel hurt, it may be a moan. Breathing deeply will help to bring us back into contact with what is happening inside of us.

If there is a great deal of anger or pain, it will benefit us to give full physical expression to that emotion in order to discharge some of the tension that has built up. One way to do this is to close ourselves in the bedroom or another private place and beat the bed with a towel or punch a pillow and throw a good temper tantrum. We might also imagine before us the person with whom we are angry and express fully everything we have wanted to say to that person. This will bring the suppressed feelings to the surface and in turn help us to be more aware of our mindtalk.

Jerry was in one of my recent Self-Esteem workshops. He claimed he already had his self-esteem, although his wife disagreed vehemently. He would not allow himself to engage in any of the emotional clearing work we did in the workshop. He would constantly cut off his feelings, staying comfortably hidden in his intellect. The idea of allowing himself to experience his emotions was actually frightening to him. He had lived a long time with the beliefs that "Men shouldn't feel," "It's not OK to show my feelings," and "If I show my feelings I will be rejected." He would not allow himself to be vulnerable and thus shut the door to his own connection with himself. Yet, each of us moves in our growth at our own pace. When Jerry is ready he will take that step toward the acknowledgment of his feelings and the freedom which that kind of honesty brings.

This denial of feelings is not uncommon, especially for men. Our culture encourages men to be strong, not emotionally clear. Experiencing one's feelings for many people is like trying to walk through a wall. Just as like poles of two magnets repel more and more strongly the closer they get, so for some people, the closer they get to their feelings, the further they want to run. Ironically, freedom is usually just the other side of that wall. Quite often it takes an act of will and courage to break through the mindtalk that says we must hide or stay away from our feelings. Yet when we do experience our feelings, we are able to do the internal work that brings about change and growth. In his evaluation of the self-esteem class, Jerry wrote, "It was good to see how much this course helped other people." For him, he was an observer, and chances are that he will remain so until he allows himself the risk, however frightening that may be, to be vulnerable and to let his true feelings be experienced.

Many of us actually live outside of our bodies. We are like people who never spend time at home. That is, when we are busy thinking about external circumstances and other people, *our awareness is not inside of us.* As we choose to take the steps to create the clarity we have always wanted in our lives, it is like going home after being away for a long time. Bringing our feelings to the surface takes the most courage and yields the most satisfying results.

When we believe our feelings are unacceptable, we often believe we will be rejected if we feel anger or hurt or embarrassment. We may even have experiences that seem to confirm these beliefs. Yet if we are to claim our self-esteem, we need to validate our feelings, even if other people around us do not. As we become grounded in our self-esteem, sooner or later our environment will begin to reflect that newfound self-acceptance. We need to practice being with ourselves and noticing what we are experiencing physically and emotionally. We need to give ourselves permission to let the tears flow, let the anger come up, and allow full expression to that which has been held deep within ourselves. As we honor our own human emotions, we unlock the door to the beliefs which must be weeded out in order to gain our freedom.

THE REPROGRAMMING PROCESS

We have spent many years listening to and acting upon our "old tapes," or old mental computer programming. A very effective way to help surface those old limiting and critical beliefs and thoughts is a technique I call the Reprogramming Process. This process is like using the "search and replace" function on a computer; *we first become aware of the negative mindtalk that has not served us; then we replace it with new thoughts that are based on loving and respecting ourselves.*

As demonstrated previously, each time an event occurs in our lives, it stimulates an interpretation of that event by our minds, which then results in whatever feelings we may have, or Event ⇨ Interpretation ⇨ Feeling. Yet, as we have noted, the interpretation is sometimes so subconscious that we do not "hear" it, which often leads us to the mistaken idea that the event causes the feelings. Therefore, to magnify the mindtalk, and thus become aware of and change our specific interpretations, we can use the Reprogramming Process.

The Reprogramming Process operates on the principle that when an event occurs, if we allow ourselves to fully experience our emotional reaction, the mindtalk will surface (Brown and Whitten, 1983). If we allow ourselves to "go inside" and be in touch with the feelings, the mindtalk becomes more "audible." Thus, because the mindtalk is not always easy to hear, we backtrack through the feelings to get to the mindtalk, It might look like this:

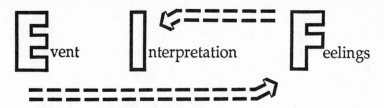

After giving full expression to our interpretation of an event (in the form of mindtalk), the next step is to review each statement in the mindtalk as to its validity, *reinterpreting* each statement in a manner that is based on the belief that we are unconditionally worthy of love and respect. Thus we replace the old belief that we are not good enough. We then complete the process with a summary statement which powerfully affirms our self-worth.

Because this process is such a valuable tool, it is suggested that this section be read slowly and with great care, perhaps even reviewing it before continuing on. The remainder of this chapter focuses on the importance and application of the Reprogramming Process. The actual steps are:

1. When an event occurs, fully experience the feelings, both emotionally and physically.
2. Listen closely to the interpretation of that event, noting specific mindtalk and beliefs.
3. Reprogram the mind by correcting each statement in the mindtalk to reflect an interpretation based on self-esteem.

1. WHEN AN EVENT OCCURS, FULLY EXPERIENCE THE FEELINGS

When we refer to an *event* in the context of the Reprogramming Process, we mean any situation to which we react with negative feelings. It may be someone cutting us off on the highway, news of layoffs at our company, or the look of annoyance on our spouse's face. If we focus fully on the event, whether it is occurring in the present or happened in the distant past, it will bring our feelings and mindtalk to the surface. Michenbaum (cited in Cormier & Cormier, 1985) suggests re-experiencing an event as if mentally replaying it like a movie. This helps us be aware that our thoughts are the link between the event and the resulting emotion. To do so, we actually put ourselves back in that situation--we see, smell, taste, touch and hear it as if it were occurring again now, recalling as many details of that moment as possible. Replaying the "movie" of that event helps us to "hear" the mindtalk.

The event to which we react can take place in a moment, in as little as a split second. It may be an expression on someone's face, a sentence that someone says, or something we see. When we "freeze-frame," or focus on the moment that caught our attention, the instant to which we reacted, our feelings will also surface, and the mindtalk will be easy to perceive.

For example, Sara was recently at a gala office party, chatting with her colleagues from the business office. They were talking about how difficult it had been to start a particular new project, and how much overtime people had put in. During the course of the conversation, the business manager said, "You certainly have a dedicated secretary. I sure wouldn't want to work forty extra hours a week for two months!" This sentence was the *event*, the moment that caught Sara's attention and stimulated her mindtalk--for her secretary had not put in much overtime at all! It was soon discovered that Sara's secretary had recently taken home an extra $2000 by adding overtime hours to her timesheet after Sara had signed it.

When Sara repeated the story about her secretary

to her friends, hurt and anger were evident in her voice. She focused the story on how much she had trusted this woman and how she had been tricked. But Sara was avoiding the real issue, her deeper concerms about her own self-worth. Finally, she chose to do the Reprogramming Process. By replaying the event in her mind and allowing her feelings to surface, Sara finally got in touch with the train of subconscious mindtalk that was causing her pain. Her interpretation of that event was, "It's all my fault, I should have supervised her better. I trusted her to take in the timesheets when I should have done it myself. I am not good at my job. I'll be fired. And, I'm not good enough."

By following the steps of the Reprogramming Process, Sara discovered that her issues were centered around her own self-esteem. When she replaced her negative mindtalk with self-esteem based statements, she reminded herself, "I am an excellent supervisor. I had no reason not to trust my secretary. My boss will not fire me, and in fact, he commended me on how I handled the situation. I was not responsible for my secretary's fraud; that was her choice of behavior. And, I am a good and valuable person."

When we decide to make use of the Reprogramming Process, we can process any event that has occurred in our lives. It can be a very traumatic experience, such as news of a loved one's accident, being asked for a divorce, or receiving physical abuse. Or the event can be a very small and seemingly insignificant incident that just barely catches our attention, such as a sideways glance, a snicker, or an almost imperceptible gesture.

The Reprogramming Process can be used for an event that has *just* happened, or we can work from an experience from our distant past. Even though it is sometimes more difficult, focusing on the painful events of our youth and childhood often helps us to access directly to the mindtalk when it first became part of the belief systems we conconsiously live by now. Once we have become proficient at reprogramming--allowing our feelings to come to the surface, listening to our interpretations of the event, and replacing them with self-esteem affirming statements--then current painful events can be processed very quickly as they occur.

John asked me to help him with the Reprogramming Process. The *issue* he wanted to work on was his difficulty in developing intimate relationships. The *event* he chose to process was his first high school girl friend's decision to break up with him. I asked John to put himself back in that scene and "replay the movie," describing it to me as if it were happening now. He said, "We are in Rhodes Park, a few blocks from the school. It's a brisk, sunny autumn afternoon. I'm walking her home from school, and she is telling me she wants to stop going together." I asked John, "What is the exact event to which you experienced a reaction?" He responded, "She says, 'You're too caring, John; I like guys who play hard to get.'" What is important to notice at this time is that the crucial event for John was only one sentence--it barely lasted three seconds--yet as we shall see later, it affected how he related to women well into his early thirties.

To fully participate in and make use of this process entails making the decision to choose clarity over the familiar old patterns or dramas of our lives. It involves jumping into that deeper work that will result in healing our thought habits and beliefs. As we allow ourselves the full exerience of the feelings at that moment of the event, we come face to face with the things we are telling ourselves about ourselves. Then, when we have brought that mindtalk or our interpretation fully to the surface, we can examine and change those beliefs and thoughts that have been limiting our lives.

2. LISTEN CLOSELY TO OUR INTERPRETATION OF THE EVENT

Once we focus fully on the feelings surrounding an event, our interpretation of that event will easily surface. Any two individuals' interpretation of an event will be different, and consequently, their mindtalk will be different. Sometimes the mindtalk will be new, specific to that event. More frequently, however, it is based on "old programming," or beliefs held since childhood. At this point in the process we do not want to analyze or in any way edit our mindtalk as it comes out, but, by staying in touch with the feelings, to vent it fully, to simply let it roll.

Some of our mindtalk will be about other people or "how the world is". But it is the negative mindtalk about ourselves--what we are, what we do right or wrong, how we should act and be, what we deserve, and whether we are good enough--which is the source of low self-esteem. Quite often, if we only allow ourselves to experience superficial levels of feelings, our mindtalk will be focused on other people. However, when we go to the depths of our feelings we will discover those beliefs that keep us from fully valuing ourselves.

As we listen to our mindtalk, it is best to write it down, listing one sentence per line as shown below. This way we can easily go back and reprogram each statement. Often people are amazed when reviewing their mindtalk later to hear what surfaced when they permitted themselves to experience their feelings. If there is someone available and willing to help facilitate the process, that person can write the mindtalk so that our own focus can be maintained on the feelings. It is important to catch each thought as it goes by. At the surface, low self-esteem mindtalk usually includes such statements as:

> I always have to dress well or I'll be rejected.
> If I'm not making $60,000 (or $15,000
>   or $200,000) a year, I'm a failure.
> I should be in a permanent relationship with
>   the perfect person right now.
> I should never be angry.
> Nothing every goes right for me.
> I'm no good at what I do.
> I never win.
> It's no use.
> If I were a good person, I would never
>   think/feel/say this
> I'm stupid.
> I'm ugly.

At a deeper level there is often:

> I'm too selfish.
> I'm responsible for other people's reactions.
> I have to keep or make other people happy.
> I'm inadequate.
> I'm not lovable.
> I'll never get what I want
> I don't deserve to be treated well.
> I'm not good enough.
> And, I'm not enough.

Sometimes there is even the belief, "I should never have been born," or, "I might as well be dead."
It is important as we listen to our mindtalk that

we do not confuse statements about feelings with the thoughts, beliefs and ideas that make up mindtalk. In the way we use language in our culture, we sometimes confuse these two, using feeling words when statements about our thoughts and beliefs are more accurate. For example, people will sometimes say, "You hurt me," "He made me angry and I feel he shouldn't do that," "I feel rejected," or "I feel justified." These are not feeling statements; they are thought statements (Brown & Whitten, 1983). They are judgments of the mind which are *based* on the feelings. If these same statements are made correctly, we separate the functions of the emotions and mind.

Instead of saying "You hurt me," we would say, "I *feel* hurt and I *think* you don't like me." Rather than "He made me angry and I feel he shouldn't do that," we would make the statement, "I *feel* angry and I *think* he shouldn't do that." "I feel rejected," would be replaced by, "I *feel* hurt and I *interpret* his actions to mean he's rejecting me." "I feel justified," would be more accurately said, "I'm *angry* and I *believe* I'm justified." When we confuse feelings and thoughts, untangling our mindtalk is almost impossible. When we accurately separate the feelings from what the mind says, we are in a position to change the old mental patterns and beliefs.

In the example above, the significant event for John was when his girlfriend said, "You're too caring; I like guys who play hard to get." John *felt* hurt, anxious, and confused. As he allowed himself to experience these feelings, he interpreted the event with mindtalk that ran as follows:

This is impossible.
I can't believe it's not OK just to love someone.
She must like someone else instead of me.

I'm not good enough for her.
I have to learn how to play the game right.
I'm going to have to pretend I don't care
    about her.
I have to make her jealous so she'll like me.
If you want to be loved, you have to try not
    to love.
I have to try not to have feelings.
I'm not OK the way I am.

When John later reviewed his mindtalk in order to reprogram it, he realized that for fifteen years he had never allowed himself to have an intimate relationship because he had believed that to be loved he had to act in a rejecting manner toward the women in his life.

Shirley was a substitute teacher who thought she was being ignored by her colleagues. For three weeks she had been trying to communicate her views with no apparent success. The event she decided to process occurred at a meeting. She was sitting at a table with the other teachers and had just stated her opinion. The *event* to which she reacted occurred at that moment: she observed her colleagues turn away from her without responding. The actual visual and auditory data of the "movie" which she re-experienced was heads turning away and conversation unrelated to her statement. She *felt* hurt, shocked, numb, anxious, and angry. By "replaying the movie" of that event and staying with the feelings as they arose, she was able to reach deeper and deeper levels of her mindtalk:

They should listen to me.
I have tried everything.
I'm inadequate.
People take advantage of me.

It's all my fault.
People don't like me.
I'm different.
I'm wrong.
I'm threatening to them.
I have to act the way they want.
It's hopeless.
I have to blank this out.
I don't deserve consideration.
I don't matter.
I'm not wanted.
I'm not good enough.

As we can see, at the surface Shirley's interpretation of that event related to other people. Only as she reached for deeper levels of her interpretation of the event did her mindtalk reflect core beliefs about her own lack of value.

It is important that constant contact with the feelings be maintained while listening to mindtalk. Sometimes we need to let the tears come up and allow the anger to be voiced. If necessary, we can mentally return to the event and again re-experience it in order to avoid "going up into the head," or logically figuring out what the mind "probably" said. The true subconscious beliefs and judgments about ourselves are accessed through experiencing the genuine feelings, thus uncovering layer upon layer of mindtalk. Toward the bottom of those layers there are always the key beliefs that are the basis of our interpretations and the cause of low self-esteem.

3. REPROGRAMMING WITH SELF-ESTEEM BASED STATEMENTS

Step three of the Reprogramming Process is to correct each statement in the mindtalk to reflect an interpretation of the event based on self-esteem rather than on self-judgment. When we begin this step of the process, we move from a perspective of being fully immersed in the feelings, beliefs and pain of our low self-esteem, into a position of objectivity. Whereas in the first two steps we absolutely wallow in the drama of our lives so we can more effectively realize the underlying beliefs, *in this portion we absolutely adhere to the truth--that we are ALL unconditionally lovable, good enough, and worthy.* We take on the perspective of the observer within, of our Higher Power or Higher Self.

When our mindtalk is running, we tend to be merciless with ourselves. As we review each line, we want to *be sure we do not allow these long-standing self-limiting beliefs to continue.* It is beneficial to remember that these beliefs have been a part of our habitual thinking for many years and they often feel true. We now reprogram the mind from the perspective, one might say, of God in all of His compassion and love. Instead of taking the "Is my glass half empty?" interpretation of events, we shift to "Wow, look at how my glass is almost full!" In other words, we change our interpretation. We take a different perspective. We shift our focus from our shortcomings (which we all have), to our strengths (which we also all have). Thus, for example, the mindtalk, "I am not adequate," is reprogrammed, and might be written as, "I am extremely adequate--in fact quite good at what I do, even though, like everyone else, I make mistakes from time to time."

It is best to take the time to examine each line of mindtalk until our reprogrammed statements have the ring of truth for us. Most criticisms--and the belief that we are "not good enough" when we do not fulfill our perfectionistic demands--are simply not the truth! *The TRUTH is, we are unconditionally lovable and worthy of esteem.* Be unwilling to allow negative thoughts about the self and others to persist. As we reprogram our minds by affirming our value and self-esteem, we will start to notice that, *as we have changed our thoughts, our feelings change as well!*

John, whose high school girlfriend left him, replaced the old thoughts with new, self-esteem based thoughts as follows: "These things happen. It's OK just to love someone. She didn't like someone else, but she was caught in some unhealthy codependent patterns. I *was* good enough for her. I don't have to play games to be loved. Being myself is better than pretending." Becoming aware of this subconscious pattern allowed John to begin to create relationships that were based on honesty and vulnerability rather than manipulation. Rather than always being concerned about how to control the other person, he could simply enjoy being himself and allow himself to be in relationships with women who liked him exactly as he was.

In reviewing and verifying our mindtalk, we go back over each statement that we made while we were attuned to the event and our feelings. What we will now notice is that our negative mindtalk is usually based on unkind criticism and unrealistic demands we have made of ourselves or others. It is important to be strictly honest with ourselves here. If we say "No one loves me", it is not a true statement. It may feel true because it is familiar, but that does not make it true. We may not always be loved in the manner that we prefer, but when we think about it, each of us knows of at least a few people who love us in some way or another. It is necessary to recognize that the bulk of the negative things we say to ourselves are simply untrue.

There are certain words that are clues to untrue

statements about ourselves that foster low self-esteem. Sometimes these words are merely implied by the context or intention of our mindtalk. Often, however, they regularly make up the way in which we phrase our mindtalk. Notice what the following words have in common:

> Should or Ought to
> Shouldn't or Ought not to
> Have to
> Can't
> Always
> Never

Each time we use one of these words, we are giving up our choices and our power. We do this by living according to the absolute rules about good and bad, right and wrong that these words imply--rather than living by making appropriate decisions and choices in the moment. Based on painful situations in the past, we make up rules that we imagine will keep us from experiencing that pain again. Or, in order to win our parents' love, we take on the absolutes that they created from their life experiences.

Once we decide that these rules are the truth, we cease to examine their validity in each situation and we simply believe we "should" or "can't" be or do something. These rules, founded on the fear of repeating past pain, become the cornerstone of many of our beliefs and the decisions we make. They are the basis of codependency. We thus give up our freedom, our choices, and the truth, in order to have feelings of safety. The mindtalk, for all practical purposes, then becomes our reality. We live and act as if those beliefs, those "have tos," "shoulds," "can'ts," and "nevers" were true. When we make our reprogramming statements to replace our old mindtalk, we take responsibility for our lives by using words such as "choose to," "want to," "choose not to," and "sometimes."

It is also important to be aware of our own resistance to change. If change were easy, we would all have done it long ago. Sometimes we can fool ourselves; at times we do not reprogram our mindtalk accurately because that would mean we would have to make major adjustments in the way we are used to living. We would have to give up familiar beliefs and lifestyles. Change is almost never comfortable. In later chapters we will look at why we keep old beliefs and habits that no longer serve us.

Other signs of resistance are when we suddenly become sleepy, blank out on part of a conversation or a part of our processing, when we need to change the subject or interrupt, or even when we suddenly need to use the bathroom. These can be little clues that there is negative mindtalk involved which we do not want to face. A person truly seeking clarity in life will use such potential indicators to discover and reprogram the deeper critical mindtalk.

If we find ourselves clinging to the old mindtalk instead of being willing to replace it with esteem-based statements, we need to check to see if we are:

1. Being willing to be completely objective,
2. Clinging to negative beliefs about ourselves or others out of habit,
3. Using "should, have to, never, can't" and other inappropriate "absolutes,"
4. Using feeling statements in the mindtalk section of the process. ("I feel angry at myself" is not mindtalk; it is a statement about a feeling. The *real* mindtalk in this situation would be, "What I did is unforgiva-

ble." This can then be reprogrammed to "I made a mistake and
now I forgive myself.")

When Shirley, the substitute teacher we discussed earlier, was ready to reprogram her mindtalk,
she gradually moved from depression and tears to
laughter as she made her new reprogramming statements, which are given in parentheses below. I have
also added my own notes to explain why some com-
monly accepted mindtalk is not accurate and needs to
be reprogrammed.

I've tried everything. (There are many things I
haven't tried; there are infinite options.)

They have to give an inch. (They don't have to
do anything, even though I wish they would.
Note: "Have to's" are almost never true
statements.)

I'm inadequate. (Actually, I do a very good job.)

People take advantage of me. (They take
appropriate advantage of the use of a
substitute teacher, but they are not trying to
abuse me, which was what I was implying.)

It's my fault. (Their behavior is their
responsibility, not mine. I was expecting the
full time teachers to make more use of my
ideas when that was not necessarily
appropriate to my role or theirs.)

People don't like me. (There are many
people who like me.)

I'm different. (I'm no more different than
  anyone else. Each of us is unique.)

I'm wrong. (I just wanted to do it differently
  from the majority; that doesn't make me
  wrong. Note: This is an important concept
  to understand when reprogramming. We
  often want to be right or to avoid being seen
  as wrong. In reality, most situations are
  truly a matter of personal opinion, values
  or preference.)

I'm threatening to them. (That's only my
  interpretation, and I may be making it up.
  I'll have to ask them in order to find out how
  they really feel. (Note: More often than not,
  if we share our mindtalk with a real desire to
  communicate, the other person will often be
  willing to help create clarity by confirming or
  correcting our interpretations of their actions
  and feelings.)

I have to act the way they want. (Another
  "have to," which is not accurate. It's OK to act
  the way I do; I'm doing the best I can. But on
  the other hand, perhaps I need more
  information of what is expected in the
  substitute teacher role.)

It's hopeless. (I change that idea by doing this
  process. Not only is there hope, but I'm seeing
  many new possibilities at this time.)

I have to blank this out. (In fact, if I blank
  it out, I won't deal with it. It's better to be
  aware of it.)

I don't deserve consideration. (I am deserving of
   consideration, even though sometimes I
   might not get it.)

I don't matter. (I do matter.)

I'm not wanted. (Actually, I am very much
   wanted in that job. But perhaps they do not
   want additional input from someone who is
   there only temporarily. This reminds me that
   I have also told myself often that even my
   parents didn't want me, so I see it's the same
   issue. It all came from one thing my mother
   said when I was four years old. And when I
   mentioned it before she died, the look
   of surprise on her face told me that it
   really hadn't been meant the way I had
   interpreted it for thirty-five years. (Note:
   Notice that in processing one event, Shirley
   is put in touch with an earlier one that
   centers around the same issue. This is not
   unusual, and it often enables us to go ahead
   and process the second one.)

I'm not good enough. (Everyone is good
   enough, including me!)

Notice what happened to Shirley as she verified
the mindtalk. She realized that "being wanted" was a
very old issue for her. Her mother's expression had
shown her that a thirty-five year old belief was not
true. She noticed that she had once again been caught
in the same belief that had often affected her relationships with others. She is now in a position to watch
for and reprogram it more quickly when it comes up

next time. As we consider the mindtalk in our own process, it helps to be clear as to why our old interpretations are untrue. This will create real perceptual shifts that are the basis of living in a new and healthier manner.

In completing the Reprogramming Process, it is a good idea to make a powerful statement that summarizes the truth of our value in relation to the event which occurred. John, whose high school girlfriend had told him he was too caring, affirmed his self-esteem by saying, "I told myself that I would be rejected if I didn't withhold my love; the truth is, it is not necessary to play such games. I can love and be loved in a open and honest manner." Shirley, the substitute teacher, completed the Reprogramming Process with "I was very much wanted in my role as a substitute teacher, although I had unrealistic expectations that they would want me to participate in their core planning. I am good at my job and my skills are appreciated."

The Reprogramming Process can be used in relation to mindtalk about others as well as ourselves. When I was a child my father would sometimes spank me quite soundly and with much anger. My mindtalk for many years was that my father is *always* abusive, and *always* angry, and that *I have* to keep him happy. I lived in constant fear of him, even as an adult, and saw few redeeming qualities in him.

Then one day I was doing the Reprogramming Process on an event where I received a severe spanking. A friend who was working with me asked, "You mean he spanked you *ALL* the time? How many times each day?" I realized that the absolutes in my mindtalk set me up to interpret my relationship with my father as completely negative. When I examined my mindtalk, I reprogrammed it to reflect a more loving--

and more accurate--picture: "Because my father punished me severely sometimes, I saw him only as being abusive. He actually loves me very much and has often been very supportive and nourishing to me." I now perceive my father as a sweet, generous and sensitive man. I treat him accordingly--and he acts accordingly. Since I was willing to change how I perceived a relationship that was antagonistic for years, I now have a wonderful relationship with my Dad.

As we use this process over and over again, we become very adept at it. After a while, when we have applied it to many similar events, we can catch the old belief system patterns as they arise. We reach a point where we say to ourselves, "Oh, it's that old one again. That's not true. I really am lovable." It becomes very easy to *nip the mindtalk at the bud before it starts a whole line of negative interpretations that interfere with our self-esteem.* In time it simply becomes a matter of changing the mindtalk--the old thought habits--which no longer serve us. If we do the Reprogramming Process regularly--daily--every time we feel upset or experience a negative emotion, it will bring us to the truth of our inherent value every time. *And the truth will set us free.*

EXERCISES

1.   Go back to the beginning of this chapter and review the steps of the Reprogramming Process. Set yourself a goal of doing this process at least once a day for one week.

2.   Copy the steps of the Reprogramming Process and keep them with you. *Any* time you feel a

negative emotion, take a few minutes, track back to the event and the feelings which surround it, and complete the process.

<u>4</u>

Getting Artificial Self-Esteem from Codependency

GROWING UP CODEPENDENT

All of us have times when we "feel bad." That is to say, we feel emotions such as hurt, anger, shame, and depression. These negative emotions are a part of life. There is no one who has the ability to avoid them. What we do with them is another matter. It is now generally accepted in psychological circles that the best way to handle feelings is to allow them expression. Hence the increased application in the last twenty years of Gestalt, Primal Therapy, The Life Training, est, Hakomi, and other cathartic approaches to emotional healing.

Expressing what is inside of us is natural. If we watch a child who has just been hit by his friend during an argument, the response is immediate and spontaneous. All of his "I don't like it" energy is given expression with every part of his body. He raises his voice, shakes his fists, cries, kicks, and lets loose of every bit of mindtalk that he can. He may even get down on the floor and pound on it with all four limbs. It is not unusual, however, to see ten minutes later contentedly engaged in playing with his friend again, oblivious to his feelings and behavior only moments before.

While this kind of expression of feelings has a wonderfully purgative effect, it obviously is unacceptable in the office after it has just been anounced that there will be layoffs next week, or at a business lunch where the client has just told you that you can't beat your competitors' product. More "appropriate" responses are made. Perhaps there are jokes or innuendos made. There may be a big smile and a cheery "I don't really care" stance taken. Or perhaps there is a determined, redoubled effort to manipulate the situation to change. Somewhere between the playground and the office, some drastic revisions in operating style occur.

Whether or not those changes in style result in a healthy way of dealing with problems depends greatly on the individual and the environment in which each of us grew up. In a healthy home, parents or other significant adults provide an environment that supports the development of self-esteem. Usually these parents also experience high self-esteem themselves; therefore, passing it on to their children is natural. Coopersmith (1981), McDonald (1980), Philips and Zigler (1980) and String (1971) have identified certain parental behaviors and attitudes which foster the development of self-esteem. A parent who teaches self-esteem will:

1. Express unconditional caring, acceptance, warmth and understanding; separate a child's behavior from who he or she is as a human being.

2. Recognize, respect and encourage individual differences.

3. Give clearly defined and enforced limits. (If the parents' value system is shifting, uncertain or in conflict, the child's sense of when he is right or wrong will be confused. Effective discipline is firm, consistent, immediate, appropriate, and gentle, so that child has a clear understanding of the relationship between actions and consequences. This also instills in the child feelings of effectiveness, safety and confidence.)

4. Listen carefully; provide opportunities for individual expression and decision-making within appropriate limits.

5. Encourage self-reliance and exploration.

6. Teach a child to capitalize on strengths rather than focus on weaknesses.

7. Respond supportively to disappointments and failures; refrain from blaming, yet not shelter the child from failure; teach coping skills.

8. Provide appropriate models with an understanding that children emulate what they see.

In contrast, when adults have not developed their own self-esteem and appropriate coping skills, clearly they have no basis for teaching this to their children. In a family that is dysfunctional, the parents' inability to appropriately express and deal with their feelings--their fears, hurts, and frustrations--will in essence be taught to their children. Their children become an extension of their egos--their own unfulfilled dreams and their own unresolved issues. If Dad repressed his anger when he was criticized for the quality of his work that day, he may rage at his son that evening for not performing better at school. If Mom is concerned with looking good in the eyes of her neighbors, she may push her daughter into social situations inappropriately early.

Parents who are not communicating well may use their children to express their anger at each other. Or, they may use their children as confidants, forcing them into the conflict of having to side with one parent or the other. We call this situation "triangulation," where parents consciously or unconsciously use their children to communicate with each other because they do not know how to communicate directly. Napier and Whitaker (1978) explain that in triangulation, two parents who are emotionally estranged over-involve their children in their own aloneness, setting up patterns that are perpetuated for generations.

When parents depend on their children to be the shock absorbers of their own unresolved issues, they teach them codependency. Rather than be a model for the belief that "I am a good and valuable person, and I have the resources to fulfill my needs," they teach their children to believe "I do not have inherent value in myself; I need someone or something else to help me feel OK."

In my private practice I see examples of this on a daily basis. Donna's mother worries constantly; she uses Donna as a sounding board for all of her concerns. Donna has come to believe that she must keep a tight lid on her thoughts and feelings lest she make her mother feel worse. But, of course, there is no amount of keeping the lid on her feelings that will help her mother feel better because her mother's worrying is habitual. Donna's mindtalk, understandably is, "I can never be enough."

Jean's father was a "womanizer." Unable to face his own guilt, he accused his wife of sleeping with other men. He focused this idea on Jean, whom he constantly called illegitimate whenever he felt angry towards his wife. Jean grew up keeping to herself and trying to stay out of the way, believing that she made her parents angry. She carried into adulthood the mindtalk that "My feelings are illegitimate; I'm illegitimate--I shouldn't even have been born."

Bill's parents rarely communicated. Over the years they developed a style of getting along that involved his dad sitting in angry silence peppered with occasional abusive outburts, while his mother prattled on in a constant drone of chitchat about surface things that had little meaning to either of them. Bill's job as a child was to help ease the tension by keeping his feelings to himself and by always looking good. He came to me when he realized he was easing out of still another meaningless relationship, one of many. His belief had always been, "It's not safe to share what's inside of me. Who I am doesn't matter; the only thing that matters is keeping things cool." This is not exactly a precursor to intimacy.

Rita's mother had always wanted to be an actress but had chosen motherhood instead. She felt like a failure because she had not pursued her dream. But she taught her daughters a great deal about acting and encouraged them to be involved in school drama productions. While Rita was very successful at it, her mother constantly cautioned her that "you can never be a success at it; it's not an appropriate career; and there are better things to do with your life." Rita became an actress, but until she sought counseling, she kept herself constantly near poverty. Her belief had been, "I can be an actress, but I can never succeed." On a deeper level she had learned from her mother, "I don't deserve to have what I want."

Beth's father was an alcoholic. While they had a fairly good relationship by day, he would become abusive in the evenings. Her mother would quietly disappear from the scene, thus her father would often focus his angry soliloquies on her. When she was in her early teens, he began frequenting bars, leaving the family fearful for his safety and constantly uncertain as to when and if he would show up. In an effort to keep him out of the bars, Beth managed at the age of twelve, to purchase liquor so that it would be available to him at home. She thus daily faced either the uncertainty of his whereabouts or an evening of verbal abuse.

Beth grew up believing, "Men are always abusive but you have to take care of them; what I need and want doesn't matter." When I first met her she worked a full time job, and in the evening took care of the housework and the children while her husband watched TV and drank beer. As she began to believe she deserved more, she gradually developed the ability to change her reality so that she received more.

MAKING CODEPENDENCY
AN ADULT LIFESTYLE

In each of the cases above, and in most dysfunctional family situations, children do not learn that they are inherently valuable and worthy. Instead they learn rules for survival, rules of how to behave to keep things from going awry, rules for getting their value by negating their own needs and/or somehow attempting to save their parents. *But because they can neither successfully negate their own needs nor save their parents, they also learn that whatever they do is "insufficient" or "not enough."* This is the core of what creates codependency. It is also the core of what creates low self-esteem.

There is a prevailing theory that says low self-esteem is a result of codependency and other addictive patterns. This may be true, however it is only true in the sense that those patterns *perpetuate* low self-esteem. *In fact, low self-esteem is usually learned first.* The codependent patterns are the result of adapting to the belief that we are not good enough. They are behaviors that are learned in an attempt to avoid the overwhelming evidence in a dysfunctional family for the belief that "I don't have worth."

Using the Event ⇨ Interpretation ⇨ Feeling model, we see that a typical occurrence in childhood is: parent expresses anger (event), child's mindtalk is that he is the cause of the anger (interpretation), child feels shame (feeling). What occurs next is the beginning of codependency. The child's feeling becomes the basis for his behavior (action). Typically, the child alters his normal behavior and attempts to do or be or feel something different in order to please the parent or avoid pain. Thus, our complete diagram now reads:

E vent ⇨ I nterpretation ⇨ F eeling ⇨ A ction

In the examples above, three of the individuals have battled alcoholism, two have abused drugs, two have struggled with overeating, three at one time smoked cigarettes, four are workaholics, and one has struggled with compulsive spending. Every one of them has struggled with issues of codependency. They learned at a very young age that codependent and other addictive behaviors would help them "feel better" when things did not go well at home.

When there is the belief that we are not enough and that we do not have value, then the concept that we can solve our own problems, fulfill our own needs, and make ourselves happy, is simply not in our mental computer. When we have low self-esteem, we do not look inside for our answers because we don't believe they are there. An image that I hear repeated over and over when people first come for counseling is that they feel empty and hollow, and that there is a big hole that they want to fill. So we look outside. We *depend* on someone or something to fill that aching hole. Thus, as has been stated before, we develop a codependent relationship with a person or substance that will, at least temporarily, fill the void and make us feel better.

But because the belief that "I'm not worthwhile" persists, the codependency also persists. The "feeling better" only lasts until the next time the thought arises, on however subconsious a level, that "I am not enough." For a woman who eats to feel better, that thought may occur with every bite, since a stream of guilt and self-criticism often accompanies every moment of binge eating. For someone who drinks, the stuffing of feelings, raging at relatives, hangover and loss of work, all bring remorse and an enormous amount of mindtalk about "what a lousy person I am," A woman who lets her husband decide everything because she wants to be taken care of and to avoid conflict, ends up berating herself for "being nothing in life."

Codependency is a stop-gap measure to create the illusion of self-esteem. It says I need someone or something else to feel complete, balanced, secure and whole. It says, "I don't have value unless someone or something else confirms that value." It looks outside for solutions to problems because it says, "There is nothing here inside."

Codependency is learned in childhood, and can be greatly magnified or embellished in adulthood. It fills that painful emptiness in the moment, but in time, becomes part of a cycle that keeps low self-esteem in place. Thus codependency soon becomes addictive or compulsive. It is up to each person to take responsibility to step out of that cycle. It takes an act of *will* to start changing codependency into self-esteem. And, the decision to do that is the first and greatest act of self-esteem, for it says, "I AM worth-while, and I am going to start learning how to treat myself accordingly."

CODEPENDENT BEHAVIORS

As was discussed in Chapter One, there are two components that require healing in order to move from codependency into self-esteem. The first, and most critical is the thoughts and beliefs about our value, that is, how we interpret the events and situations in our life. Changing our thoughts is the most important because everything we create in our lives originates in thought.

Yet, becoming aware of our habitual behavior patterns and discovering more effective ways of living and relating are also important. *We cannot change something unless we are aware of it.* Thus, it is necessary to look at how codependency manifests, what the typical feelings and behaviors are, and what we get out of perpetuating the codependent cycle. The following are eleven basic aspects of codependency and why we keep them going.

THE CODEPENDENCY CHAIN

1. Believing we are not enough.
2. Fear of abandonment and fear of being alone.
3. Choosing a partner, substance, or behavior based on filling the emptiness.
4. Giving in order to get.
5. Giving our own power to others.
6. Attempting to regain power by caretaking, dominating, manipulating, or avoiding: taking control in disguise.
7. Feeling consumed and losing a sense of one's self
8. Lack of ego boundaries.
9. Wanting unconditional love but not giving it.
10. Fear of risk, change, and letting go.
11. No true intimacy: refusal to commit to another and perpetuation of the pattern.

---

1. Believing we are not enough.

When we believe we are not enough, not sufficient, inadequate, unlovable, and all the other negative thoughts that we have about ourselves, we put the codependency chain in operation. Since we believe that our value is based on fulfilling certain conditions, our energy is spent on living up to those standards rather than taking care of our selves and living a creative life. If we think we are not enough, we think we have to do something to be enough, rather than to simply live by our choices and our preferences. Thus low self-esteem sets us up for codependent and other addictive behaviors.

2. Fear of abandonment and fear of being alone.

When we are codependent, we believe that any love we receive is conditional upon what we can do to keep another person happy. Therefore, since we do not see ourselves as essentially lovable, we experience being at constant risk of abandonment. Often this fear is based on having been abandoned as children. Sometimes the abandonment was physical, as in divorce. Often, however, we were emotionally abandoned. If parents are preoccupied with their own problems, the children's need for love and support may not be met. Whether children are criticized or abused, or whether they are given to believe that their feelings don't count, the net effect can be that they face many of the major crises of childhood alone.

Being alone is often very frightening when we are codependent. It confirms our worst fears. If we do not fill our time with busy work, food, alcohol or fantasy, we are left to face our own minds and the reality we have created. Since we do not believe we are lovable or worthy of respect, we do not love or respect ourselves. "Alone" time is often spent in self-critisism, which can lead to depression. Thus, alone time can be doubly devastating if it is spent in negative mindtalk, for 1) it can appear to confirm that we are not wanted by others and 2) it can also be spent in listening to our own criticisms of ourselves. Filling that empty hole becomes imperative in order to feel better.

3. Choosing a partner, substance, or behavior based on filling the emptiness.

When we are codependent, we believe we do not

deserve love and support. We therefore often settle for any companionship to avoid facing the pain of loneliness, even if that companionship is abusive or unhealthy. We may move from one relationship directly into another to avoid ever being alone. Or we may marry early "just to get out of this hellhole," only to find ourselves in another one. If the relationship we choose for filling the emptiness is not with a person, it can just as easily be with food, alcohol, TV, or any other compulsive behavior.

As codependents, we choose partners based on our deficits and our unmet needs. A man who is afraid of being powerless may marry a woman who is afraid of making decisions. He trades taking care of her for being able to have the power. Yet neither is happy, for he gets tired of taking responsibility for her as if she were a child, and she resents never having anything her way. A woman who is afraid of giving up her independence may have a relationship with a man who is afraid of making commitments. She gets her freedom; he gets to avoid intimacy. But neither is happy because they are both lonely. A man who is grouchy and negative marries a woman who is always cheerful and never expresses her negative feelings. He gets to vent his anger and she gets to see herself as a good and saintly person. But neither is happy because he has never learned to express his positive side and she has never allowed herself to be honest about her negative side.

We all tend to repeat what we learned in childhood. Whatever patterns are familiar, they are almost universally repeated in adulthood until such time as they are identified and changed. Even then, they may reappear disguised in a different form. Sonia's father was an alcoholic who constantly corrected her and told her she was bad. She married a man who was not a drinker. He had not come from an alcoholic family, but his father had always criticized him for not being a *man*. They both became deeply involved in a church which was very focused on sin, and which socially ostracized members who did not appear to measure up spiritually. There they both tended to believe again that they were not good enough. Until they got counseling, they had no idea that they had repeated their childhood patterns. (They soon switched to a church that focused more on love.)

4. Giving in order to get.

If we think we are worthless, then we believe we don't deserve. Since we believe we are not inherently deserving, then we think we have to pay for what we get--either in advance, or as retribution. Often we will "do and do and do" for another person--or our job--immersing ourselves in workaholic behavior, unconsciously thinking that this earns us the right to get the acknowledgment or nurturing back that we want. But it doesn't always work, and the results can be hurt, anger, and bitterness. At other times we may feel that our partner (child, friend, job) has not filled our emptiness sufficiently, and we may strike out in anger or resentment. Either way, rather than taking responsibility for filling our own needs, we give in order to get.

Part of our codependency involves a trade where, "I will help you maintain your illusion of self-esteem if you will help me maintain mine." In a healthy relationship the giving is from the heart and is fairly balanced between two people. In a codependent relationship, giving is part of a carefully measured barter, and both partners sooner or later feel cheated. This is because the trade almost always involves giving up a piece of our self-esteem. We stretch beyond what serves us, "sacrificing" so that we can get the other person to help us feel better, but in the process we abandon our own needs.

5. Giving our own power to others

When we choose partners based on filling that empty feeling inside instead of mutual sharing, we give our power away. We give away the control over our lives to someone or something else. We do this because there is a deep desire that the other person take responsibility for us. We want the "other" to be the loving parent we always wished we had. When we do not see ourselves as having the resources to make us happy, we give that job to our partners. Sometimes we also give it to our friends, our jobs, food, alcohol or drugs. We pepper our language with "can'ts" and "have-tos" in constant confirmation of our lack of power.

Unfortunately, in order to make another person, substance, or habit responsible for us, we also give up responsibility for ourselves. This often means giving up or compromising our feelings, thoughts, values, preferences, choices, even our identity. It also means giving up our growth, for to stay in the mutual trade-off of the codependent patterns, each must give tacit agreement not to upset the delicate balance of shared illusory self-esteem.

6. Attempting to regain power by caretaking, dominating, manipulating, or avoiding: taking control in disguise.

Clearly we can never be satisfied with giving our power away. Giving our power to another person is part of the trade-off to get the illusion of self-esteem. But the illusion is a thin veil, for feeling powerless does nothing but confirm our belief that we lack value. So we must do something to regain it. But generally this coup needs to be disguised or it will destroy the balance of the trade. Depending on the particular way that we play into the codependent dance and the tacit agreements we've made, we will generally take one of four primary approaches--caretaking, dominating, manipulating or avoiding. Each one is an indirect way of controlling the other person. These are very similar to four styles of communicating identified by Virginia Satir (1983), that is, placating, blaming, being super-reasonable, and being irrelevant. We might also notice their similarity to the four roles which children often play in a dysfunctional family: the hero, scapegoat, lost child and clown.

Perhaps the most clever way of controlling is *caretaking*. It may involve cooking and cleaning for our partners, managing their business, rescuing them from their failures, or giving them all manner of good advice. It is well diguised as being in the best interest of the other. It looks and often feels loving. It also offers the caretaker "secondary gains", or the "benefit" in the illusion of self-esteem, for it fosters the belief that "If I help people, then I'm good." What we also do when we are caretakers, however, is to constantly send the other people in our lives the message that they are not sufficient, which is why we have to be helping them all the time. Cute device, *n'est pas?* (If you are chuckling right now, you may be recognizing this as your specialty.)

A more obvious control device, but one which is less obviously codependent, is *dominating*. If we use dominating to control, we are blustery and demanding, make decisions for others, may be a "rage-aholic," and insist on getting our way. We keep others dancing in order to avoid our outburts. We are likely to pair up with caretakers; it makes a good trade. It looks as if we're in charge, and quite often demonstrates that we can handle a great deal of responsibility, for it reinforces the belief that "I am powerful." But at the same time we are aware that the other people are barely "putting up with us," which fosters the continuation of low self-esteem. And in the meantime, the message to the others is that their feelings and thoughts aren't important, which is why we have to take charge.

Manipulating and *avoiding* are both less direct approaches to controlling. When we manipulate, we attempt to deal with others by analyzing and discovering what makes them tick. We then capitalize on our knowledge of their strengths and their weaknesses to get what we want. When we practice avoiding, on the other hand, we simply will not engage with others. We control them by not dealing with their concerns. Both styles create the illusion of self-esteem because we can tell ourselves "I'm a good person because I'm calm and controlled." It is a double-edged sword, however, for we end up with our feelings iced over, making it difficult to engage in any meaningful way with another. As manipulators we give out the message, "You are too stupid to be worthwhile." In avoiding we imply to others, "What is important to you is not worth my involvement."

7. Feeling consumed and losing a sense of one's self.

As might be imagined, the drama which revolves around the codependent's attempt to maintain the illusion of self-esteem is quite exhausting and confusing. Because, as codependents, we begin with the premise that we are not acceptable the way we are, much of our energy is focused around being something else. We reject what is really going on with us and attempt to live a life based on how we "should" be. We put a tight lid on feelings that we think we should not have, such as anger, jealousy, or hurt. We act in ways that are not in alignment with our feelings, values, needs or preferences. If we do allow ourselves any of these "unacceptable" emotions or actions, we either disguise them or we are ashamed for not fulfilling the unrealistic demands we place on ourselves. Even if we are codependents who use dominating as a way to control, we may *appear* to be expressing our feelings, but we are not, for the blustery exterior covers deep hurts and the fear of being weak.

In losing touch with what is going on within us, we lose touch with our source, our means to healing. We have all seen someone seethe through clenched teeth, "I am NOT angry," or watched someone smile brightly while looking through sad eyes. Often, when I first work with a client, I find we must first peel away the layers of "how I *should* be" so we can get to *what is really inside*. The only raw material we can use for healing is who we honestly are. The cover-ups we use to create the illusion of self-esteem only obscure that diamond in the rough that we all are. As codependents, the greater that cover-up is, and the more we turn our power over to others, the more lost we feel. And it is no wonder, for we have entirely buried ourselves in an intricate drama that bears no relation to who we really are.

8. Lack of ego boundaries.

It is a natural corollary that when we have lost contact with ourselves, we also lose track of our ego boundaries. What this means is, "I don't know where I stop and you begin." Codependents regularly take inappropriate responsibility for each other. Quite often the man will take physical responsibility for the woman, while the woman takes emotional responsibility for the man, although there are many other possible trade-offs. A woman who feels powerless may defer disciplining the children to Dad--when he gets home. Single parents often lean on the eldest child for support, weakening the appropriate parent-child relationship and requiring that child to take emotional responsibility for the parent. One spouse often plays the child role while the other plays the adult, each requiring the other to give up an important part of the self in order to keep the roles functioning.

When we lack ego boundaries we can: allow others to make decisions for us, allow others to speak for us or interrupt us, do things we don't want to because someone else wants us to, including have sex when we don't wish to, spend time with people we don't want to be with, repress our own feelings so others can express theirs, allow people to do things which hurt us, blame ourselves, not defend or stand up for ourselves--and/or we can impose all of those conditions on someone else. While losing ego boundaries often happens in childhood, the accompanying behaviors are carried over into adulthood. When we are accustomed to allowing someone else to take responsibility for a certain part of us, we seek out an adult partner who will continue to fill that void. It thus becomes obvious why dysfunction gets passed from generation to generation.

9. Wanting unconditional love but not giving it.

When we believe ourselves to be worthless and unlovable, our only hope to be loved is by the prince charming or fairy princess of our dreams. We cannot imagine being in the kind of healthy relationship in which both partners constantly work to make it good. Instead, our "can'ts," "shoulds," and "have-tos" give us permission to avoid change. We want our partner to take up the slack, to save us, as it were, from our own negative beliefs about ourselves. In essence, this means we require unconditional love from our partner, and we are indignant, hurt, and/or angry when we do not receive it. This, of course, adds to our already massive belief that we are not good enough.

At the same time, we cannot give unconditional love because we *need* our partners to fill our emptiness. To do this they must do certain, specific things that help us to feel better. Thus, our love is conditional. It is also conditional for one other important reason: *we cannot give what we do not have.* Because we have not learned to love ourselves unconditionally-- we do not accept our weaknesses and errors--then we usually don't know how to do that for another person.

10. Fear of risk, change, and letting go.

When our illusion of self-worth is bolstered and supported by the delicate house of cards that we have discribed above, and when upsetting that balance means breaking unspoken trade agreements, it is clear that any deviation from very specified roles becomes threatening. What is known may not be comfortable, but at least it is familiar. It offers a kind of security.

When one person in a couple decides to step out of the codependent patterns and create self-esteem, it is a very risky step. On one hand, it may lead to the break-up of the relationship and the frightening prospect of life alone or supporting children alone. If we remain in the relationship, we are still faced with the possibility of going at the growth process alone if our partner is in denial about the need for change. We also may have to face our partner's anger and resistance when we disengage from the roles and rules by which we have lived. If we are lucky, we have a partner who wishes to share the growth process, but even that is frightening, for it involves charting new territory for both. Claiming our own self-esteem means letting go of the need to control the other person in order to get that illusion of self-worth. It means being vulnerable and courageous. For many codependents, this poses a serious question: are those risks worth the freedom? Am I willing to take those risks in order to see myself as a worthy and valuable person?

11. No true intimacy; refusal to commit to another and perpetuation of the pattern.

When we are not acceptable to ourselves, we certainly cannot imagine we will be acceptable to another. Therefore, the parts we don't like about ourselves remain our deep, dark secrets. We would never reveal them to another person. Sometimes they are even secrets from ourselves. When we are too ashamed or fearful about what is inside to look at it ourselves or to expose it to another person, we cannot be completely open and honest. We can only show parts of ourselves, and much of our energy is spent covering up who we really are. What we are willing to expose is an image of what we *think* is good enough coupled with fluff--the cover-up.

When we are codependent, we may share a home and we may share our bodies, but we do not share ourselves. When we communicate, we keep what's really true and important to us to ourselves. In essence, we avoid intimacy. In *Healing The Child Within*, Charles Whitfield (1987) says that the codependent self is a false self, a cover-up, forever inhibited, frightened, and withholding. It is other-oriented, always planning, denying feelings, confirming, and giving love only conditionally.

Sharing ourselves means risking, being vulnerable and being honest. It means that being who we are is more important than looking like someone who doesn't even exist. When we have created our relationships based on our whole selves--the bad with the good--we are in a position to make a commitment, for all the cards are on the table. When we withhold the parts of ourselves which we do not honor, we can neither trust ourselves to enter into a commitment, nor can we trust another. Thus we lock ourselves into our codependent patterns in our relationships and, as such, pass codependency on to our children.

If all of the above seems a bit frightening or overwhelming, keep in mind that the journey of a thousand miles begins with the first step. We cannot change patterns that we do not see. Some say ignorance is bliss. Perhaps it would be more accurate to say that when we are ignorant, we can avoid taking responsibility for ourselves. In a way this is easier, but we all know painfully well that it is far from blissful. Once we see our patterns, it may *seem* as if we are worse off, because we see all the work that is laid before us. But it is also true that we have finally taken the most important step--identifying what has not worked well in our lives and why. The rest is a matter of putting forth the effort to change. It's a life-long process, but we're worth it.

EXERCISES

1.   Read through the codependent behaviors 1 through 11 listed above. Write a paragraph about how you participate in each behavior. Be specific, listing names, relationships and examples in each situation.

2.   Review numbers 5 and 6 above. List ways you give away your power and covertly take it back.

5

Getting Off
The Treadmill Of
Low Self-Esteem

HIDING IN THE CAGE

If having low self-esteem sometimes feels like being on a treadmill, perhaps that is because the analogy is quite appropriate. We are like a little mouse inside a steel cage, running on an endlessly turning steel wheel. We race as fast as we can, trying desperately to get away from our own criticisms that pursue us. At the same time we race toward unrealistic perfectionistic goals that elude us. Yet we get nowhere. Ironically, the cage door is open. All the mouse has to do in order to have a much more interesting, creative and exciting life is to stop running on the wheel and walk out the door. But he is oblivious to this easy exit. He is so accustomed to life on the wheel that making the choice to stop is more frightening than the prospect of spending the rest of his life running in meaningless circles.

Low self-esteem is the cage we put ourselves in when we believe we are not good enough. The door out is the truth: that we *are* good enough, that we *are* deserving, that we *are* capable, that we *are* lovable. Yet what keeps us running in circles is our specific judgmental mindtalk and the negative feelings we have as a consequence of that mindtalk.

The judgmental mindtalk falls into two primary categories. Either we are *critical* of ourselves, calling ourselves all manner of nasty things, or we *demand* perfection of ourselves, relentlessly pushing ourselves to be different from how we are (Brown & Whitten, 1987). Together these two categories create a cycle which perpetuates low self-esteem. When something doesn't go the way we want, we criticize ourselves. Once we have thus judged ourselves, we then demand of ourselves that we fulfill absolute standards. However, being human, we clearly cannot meet those perfectionistic standards. Thus failing at an impossible goal, we once again criticize ourselves.

For example, Jason criticized himself, labeling himself as unlovable. He therefore demanded that he always do what other people wanted. Since this caretaking approach brought him some friends, but no real intimacy, he also criticized himself for not being handsome enough. This led him to another demand, which was that he had to work out with weights and exercise several hours a day so he would have a perfect physique. This did bring him more female attention, but not of the quality he wanted, so he criticized himself for not being wealthy enough. He then demanded of himself that he stay in an extremely lucrative position that he, nonetheless, did not enjoy. And so it goes.

Linda's mindtalk took her in a different direction. Because she criticized herself as a bother to others and not good enough, she demanded of herself that she never create any waves. She went to great lengths to dodge anything that had a hint of conflict. This avoiding style kept her out of trouble, but resulted in a self-criticism that she was a powerless weakling. To counter this mindtalk, she had a subconsious demand that she look bigger to people--and she ate a lot. As we might imagine, she criticized herself for being a pig. This resulted in feelings of anger toward herself, and in demanding that she feel better, she ate even more. And so it goes.

Criticism, demand, criticism, demand, criticism--we keep racing around the wheel of low self-esteem. With our criticisms we brand ourselves as unworthy; with our demands we desperately race toward an unattainable goal in an attempt to avoid the criticisms we have leveled against ourselves, only to be disappointed and to return again to yet another criticism. Around and around the cage we race, unfulfilled and exhausted by the effort.

It may be evident in the two examples above that the train of thought had a great resemblence to the negative mindtalk which surfaces in the Reprogramming Process. Indeed, that Process facilitates bringing our subconscious criticisms and demands to our awareness. Mindtalk about ourselves that fits into the criticism category tends to start with "I am," "I am a," "I am too," "I can't," or "I never." For example, we say to ourselves, "I'm a fool, I'm ugly, I'm too weak, I can't ever be happy, and I never do anything right." Mindtalk in which we make demands of ourselves often starts with "I have to," "I should," "I shouldn't," "I ought to (not to)." Examples of demands we make on ourselves are, "I have to keep everyone happy, I should work hard all the time, I shouldn't show my anger (or even feel anger), I ought to have a cleaner house, and I have to be perfect."

We all have our own special list of criticisms and

demands. Here is a portion of Jeanne's list. She had recently experienced an event where she had been called to her son's school because of his behavior problems. Reading across, the cyclical nature of the mindtalk becomes apparent.

CRITICISMS	DEMANDS
It's my fault he's in trouble	I should never let him misbehave
I'm too lenient	I have to discipline him more
I don't know how to make him behave	I should be able to make him mind me
I'm not strong enough	I have to get his Dad to discipline him
I'm too weak	I have to pretend it's the man's job
I'm a failure	I have to drink to feel better
I'm worthless	I have to cover my feelings by drinking more

Until Jeanne did the Reprogramming Process, she did not realize she was telling herself a series of false statements that perpetuated her low self-esteem. She thought she had no choices and was not aware that her criticisms and demands were making things worse instead of better. When Jeanne reprogrammed her negative mindtalk, she realized she was not responsible for her son's behavior, but that she *could* get some professional help to learn more effective ways of guiding him. She also decided that it was alright to feel weak sometimes, and that she was still a very worthy person.

Ironically, we participate in this cycle of criticisms and demands in an attempt to create self-esteem. We stay on the treadmill believing it will help us to feel good and to see ourselves as good people. We think if we can only fulfill our demands for perfection, then we will be "good enough." According to Nathaniel Branden (1983), we perpetuate this "pseudo-self esteem" to protect ourselves from anxiety and to provide an illusion of security while we avoid facing the real causes of low self-esteem. Thus, rather than deriving our value from believing in ourselves, we maintain a false sense of our value by attempting to live up to standards such as being dutiful, stoical, successful or attractive.

Sometimes we can do a rather good job of fulfilling these demands--at least for a while. Most of the codependent behaviors discussed in chapter four are attempts to fulfill our demands to be or look like we're acceptable, adequate, okay or good enough. If we can just work hard enough, caretake enough, dress well enough, stuff our feelings enough, take something to make us relax enough, smile enough, push people around enough, look rich enough, look unthreatening enough--then we can respect ourselves sufficiently so as to not judge ourselves ever again. However, each of those behaviors means either denying some part of ourselves or living up to unrealistic expectations--trying not to be who we are. Thus we end up sooner or later criticizing ourselves once again. The only relief from this cycle occurs when we make the choice to step off the treadmill and be kind to ourselves.

THE RULES WE LEARNED
WHEN WE WERE LITTLE

We did not mean to get on the treadmill of low self-esteem, and we are not wrong for having done so.

We learned it from our parents who learned it from their parents. We adopted our cages as a protection from the confusions and hurts in the world. We did so in order to get by, to survive, to be happy. We did it in order to create a world for ourselves which made sense, a world in which we were good in the face of evidence that we weren't.

Growing up in a dysfunctional family we learned very early that we were not inherently valuable, that we did not inherently deserve to be treated well. We learned that there were *rules* and *conditions* for being loved or accepted. If we fulfilled those conditions, we were good enough. That is, we received *conditional* love. If we did not follow the rules, we seemed to invoke anger, coldness, or some other form of punishment or abuse.

In some perspectives it may be said that our parents shamed us. A more accurate portrayal may perhaps be that our parents lived out the dysfunction they learned from their parents, and we inherited the system. We learned such generational rules as "Never speak about father's drinking; everyone must look happy at all times; if Johnny takes the flack, Mom and Dad won't fight so much; Mother is weak so the oldest has to be strong; boys have to be tough; and children are a lot of trouble." Such rules ultimately lead to repression of feelings, separation, guilt and lack of intimacy (Satir, 1983).

The results of such unspoken rules were that we, like our parents, felt ashamed of ourselves and thought of ourselves as lacking value. Nonetheless, as we grew older, the things our parents told us when our behavior was not acceptable became in time our own judgments of ourselves. What we learned to do as children in order to avoid our parents' rejection then became the demands we put on ourselves.

Tarmara came from an upper middle class highly educated, but emotionally distant family. The rules she learned there resulted in *demands* of herself that she must always be doing something constructive, that she should keep everything and waste nothing, that emotions should never be displayed, that the only way to deal with feelings is to avoid them and keep busy, and that she was a good person if she helped people and attended church often. Although she was very vivacious and intelligent, she believed she should never look too pretty or sexy lest she appear immoral, and that the woman's place is in the home. She often *criticized* herself as having nothing important to do, as being too intelligent for her own good, and as being a terrible housewife and mother. She called herself ugly, slow, dowdy, useless, and messy.

Jon was the eldest of four brothers. His father had died when he was ten. His mother had shut down her own emotions, "girded up her loins," and "put her nose to the grindstone" to manage raising four small children. Jon learned to *demand* of himself that he never need or want anything from his mother (or any woman), that he be strong and keep his feelings to himself, that he was responsible for keeping order, that he should work and never rest, and that he should take a little drink from time to time to help him overcome any feelings that might sneak to the surface. He *criticized* himself for being unable to keep order, for getting too upset when things started to fall apart, for having too many of his own needs, and (as a child trying to fill an adult's role), never being sufficient to the job at hand.

Tamara and Jon got married. The rules their children learned were based on the combination of the rules their parents learned. They had *demands* that included: men have to be in control, women should never feel fulfilled, one can only work and never rest, save everything but never have anything that is very nice, and, a little drink from time to time helps to take the pressure off. Despite the many talents and skills that ran in the family, Jon and Tamara's children tended to *criticize* themselves for being too emotional, incapable of doing enough well enough, of being unattractive, of being out of control, and of being a failure. Thus their demands and criticisms, like their genes, reflected a combination of the input from both of their parents.

Sometimes children have to try to make sense of conflicting family rules. When we are forced to choose between our parents, or between opposing values or demands that our parents have, we are in a double bind or "catch-22" situation. This only reinforces the belief that "I am not good enough" since fulfilling conflicting rules is usually impossible. This is particularly true when family rules change according to the mood of the parents. It is also true when parents manipulate each other by communicating through their children, or in the case of divorce where each parent attempts to win the affection of the children by criticizing the other parent. In this type of scenario, the children are triangulated, placed by the parents in the center of their conflict. In such situations, one of the parents may be the winner, but the children are always the losers.

Suzie's mother was ninth in a tumultuous family of ten, and she had always wanted out. Her father was a quiet man who from childhood had to work hard for survival. When the stresses of finance and family life pressed on Suzie's parents, they did not develop a means of communication, but rather her father drank and her mother wanted to get away and better herself. When Suzie was in her early teens, her mother left their farm and got a job in the city where she could attend college. In an argument that ensued while her father was helping her mother move, her mother turned to Suzie and asked *her* to make the decision as to whether or not her mother "should be allowed her freedom."

This event was not unlike many others where Suzie had been used as a pawn in her parent's communication--or lack thereof. She had often driven her father home from the local bar where he had stayed until late in order to avoid his wife's constant criticism. And, Suzie had often comforted her mother, listening to her for hours as she bemoaned her fate being married to a drunk who scarcely could provide for the family.

On the day she was asked to make her mother's decision, Suzie could not bring herself to say that her mother should not have her freedom. Suzie lived for years, as many children do, believing that she was responsible for her parents' divorce. The rules she learned were that men are irresponsible, that women have to get away from men to live a satisfying life, and that men and women cannot be happy together. She criticized herself for being unlovable and insufficient, and demanded that she always take responsibility for others and their feelings, put her own feelings aside, and that she be independent and financially successful.

GIVING UP THE FAMILY RULES

It becomes apparent from the examples above why the untruths contained in much of our mindtalk seem so very true to us. Our very perception of life itself is based on the rules that we learned at a very early age. Even when we are able to intellectually recognize that such mindtalk is false, it nonetheless means rearranging a perspective that we have had about our lives for many, many years. Clearly this rarely happens overnight. It takes constant practice. Each time we respond to an event in our old habitual manner, we have a new opportunity to examine it and tell ourselves the truth. When we are experiencing negative feelings, chances are that we are buying into that old system that no longer serves us.

As was mentioned before, the old system was based on survival, on making sense out of the particular beliefs that each of our parents contributed to our view of ourselves and our world. It is important to recall that there were many wonderful and interesting things we learned in that system--things that today help to make us the special people we each are. Part of our healing includes remembering and acknowledging the good times. At the same time, there are parts of those old perspectives that have ceased to serve us. That system, if we grew up in a dysfunctional family, was based, at least to some extent, on a codependent relationship with our parents. This is why we gave up our opinions, our personal expression, our ideas, our preferences, our feelings, and even our values. It was a trade for receiving our parents' love and approval.

What is crucial to remember here is that what we often traded for approval was core to ourselves. We traded our belief in and reliance on ourselves. Unless we were lucky enough to have parents who encouraged us to have our own opinions and who accepted our feelings, *we were faced with choosing between our own perspective and their acceptance.* The more dysfunctional the family, and the more needful we were of love, the greater our willingness to compromise our sense of self. And, without a clear idea of who we are--without the concept that we are worthy of love, acknowledgment and respect, regardless of others' needs and values--we cannot have self-esteem.

In order to get off the treadmill and step out of our cages, we must make a declaration of independence. This does not mean we have to reject our families or their values. It does not mean we have to straighten out our parents or convince them of their errors. Nor does it involve having to prove that our views, ideas, and needs are valid to anyone else. It simply means we must take responsibility to honor ourselves--unconditionally.

To do this, we shift our focus from getting the others to "treat us right" to simply making our own choices based on what we feel, need, want and like. This may or may not involve spending time with different people than we have until now. It does mean, however, that we accept ourselves as we are, even if no one else does. Of course, once we do this for ourselves, the other people around us also tend to accept us, although they may not do so right away. But this initial step means risking. It means "I choose to honor and take responsibility for myself first." It means choosing to have self-esteem.

STARTING AT THE BEGINNING INSTEAD OF THE MIDDLE

The first step in creating self-esteem in our lives is to start where we are. One would think that this would be fairly obvious, but in fact, it rarely is. How often do we find ourselves saying, "If only I had more money, then I could afford to relax more," or "If only people weren't so power-hungry, then I could do what I want," or "If only my spouse would take more responsibility, then I could stop having to work two jobs," or, "If only I were more attractive, then I would have more friends."

The premise here is that if we, or others, or circumstances were different, we could be happier. It is based on the low self-esteem *belief* that "I am not adequate enough to provide my own solutions", and it operates out of the codependent *habit* of making someone else responsible for our actions and choices. When we base our happiness on things being different from the way they actually are, we are giving away our power. We are reinforcing the belief that "I am not enough; I do not have the resources within me to live my life the way I want".

Lillian was a delightful and cultured lady who, in her late fifties had returned to graduate school so that she could get into the oil business. In her early sixties, just after she finished school, she suffered several health setbacks. In what was to be the simple correction of a deviated septum, she was oversedated, which left her in a fog for months. She had told the physician who performed the surgery that he should do whatever was needed to help her breathe better. His interpretation was that she needed extremely large nostrils, so that in addition to not having all of her mental facilities after the surgery, she was faced with the shock of now looking in the mirror at a very large nose.

Then, several months later, while working in her garden, she had her first attack of asthma. From that time on, Lillian spent years going from doctor to doctor, trying various machines and medicines, but never experiencing any relief in her constant struggle to breathe and to feel well. She almost never slept soundly. When Lillian first started coming to see me, she looked very frail. Her hands often shook; her voice was weak and halting and was interrupted by frequent efforts to draw in air. She could have been ninety rather than sixty-four. She wanted a job in the oil business and wanted me to help her see what was blocking her from obtaining one.

Lillian wanted to enter a field where much younger, skilled, experienced professionals were at the time being laid off from their jobs by the hundreds. In addition, she wanted this job, despite the fact that she was one year from retirement age and that her physical presentation was one of debility rather than ability. She kept saying, "If I could just find the right doctor.... If I could just get my desk cleared so that I could start writing applications.... If I could just get a good night's sleep so I could have the energy to apply for jobs...."

What Lillian wanted to do was to start where she wanted to be instead of start where she was. Our first task together was to help her move from demanding of herself that she have a job, into reckoning with the truth--that her chances of being hired by an oil company were so miniscule that her time and energy would be much better spent focused on what she could do instead of what she obviously couldn't. As Lillian gradually gave up living in the fantasy of her hopes and wishes, she repositioned herself in a perspective that allowed her to make many creative and exciting choices about her life based on reality. By acknowledging the limitations of the oil business at the time and her own physical limitations, Lillian found that she could make a very nice income for herself as a personal consultant to other older people who wanted to be invoved in oil leasing on a small scale. In addition, as she removed the stress of insisting that things be different from the way they were, her asthma improved dramatically.

Things are the way they are. If we start with that premise, we can, as the "Serenity Prayer" says, change the things that are within our power to change, practice letting go of that which is not within our realm of control, and have the wisdom to know the difference. If we are in denial about our limitations, then we don't have all of the puzzle pieces as we go about making improvements in our lives. Sometimes we pretend we are not angry or hurt or afraid when we are. Or we insist on the illusion that we can make other people be different when we cannot. At times we persist in the demand that we be perfect when we all make mistakes. When we live under these false notions, we are constantly frustrated because we are demanding that things be different from their reality.

Things are the way they are. We can caretake, dominate, manipulate, and avoid, we can stomp and cry, plead and pray, visualize and affirm *all we want*—it won't force things that are not under our control to be different. People and circumstances have a frustrating propensity to follow their own agendas without any regard for ours. We cannot even *force ourselves* to be different. Ask anyone with an ulcer. How long have we each been working on some form of psychological and spiritual growth? It's a stubbornly slow process. And yet we want it different and we want it NOW.

Life is full of ups and downs. We get a raise, we get laid off, our spouse brings us home a surprise, our spouse gets a lover, we get pneumonia, grandpa dies, a child breaks a leg, we make a big breakthough at a codependency meeting, we get angry, we feel hurt, someone gives us flowers. Sometimes life is the way we'd like it to be, sometimes it's not. Yet when we have an inner demand that circumstances be the way we want them to be instead of the way they are, we actually increase our pain. For example, when we feel frustration and demand of ourselves that we not feel that, we then direct anger towards ourselves. This adds more negative feelings to the frustration we already feel. In denying the way it is, we make it worse. We usually do this with mindtalk about how we "should" or "have-to" or "can't" be. *Instead of accepting things as they are, we add to our already existing pain the pain of wanting it different.*

When "how it is" falls far short of "how I want it to be," if we insist that it be different by "stuffing" our feelings, attempting to control others, or criticizing ourselves, it adds more frustration and pain to the situation. When we embrace "how it is" and whatever unpleasant circumstances and emotions that are involved, we thus honor ourselves and our reactions. In doing so we move through "how it is" with much greater ease, which actually has the net effect of improving our situation.

The pain in our lives brings us messages about the things we are doing that don't work. It is like the red light on the dashboard of our car that says "something is wrong under the hood--check and make adjustments." When we *honor* the pain--the bad days, the broken relationships, the backaches, the angry feelings--we can listen to the messages that the pain brings us. Then we can listen to the mindtalk and notice where we are not in alignment with the truth.

Let us say, for example, we have a headache. If we allow ourselves to feel it fully, giving it all our attention, we can actually listen to what it is saying to us. Sometimes it helps to actually give form to what we are "hearing." We might imagine the shape, size, color, texture, and even the sound of the headache (Brown & Whitten, 1983). If we focus on it for a few minutes, we might even notice if there is a sentence it wants to say to us. When I take clients through this procedure, quite often they discover statements such as "I need a rest!" or "I don't want to do this," or "I should like this and I don't"--messages, like the oil light on the dashoard, that need to be noticed. Once the physical and emotional discomforts are acknowledged, they can give us important data for our lives, even if it is something simple such as "Time to take a break," or "This isn't working; I think I'll try something different."

Pretending things are different keeps them the way they are, for we make our choices based on how we wish it were instead of how it is. Honoring how it is gives us the real data by which we can make our decisions and choices. How often do we enter relationships or agreements with the idea that we'll have to get that other person to change, only to find out ten years down the road that that hope was an illusion.

The paradoxical truth is that accepting things as they are opens a space for them to change. A friend once said, "You might as well accept people the way they are because that's the way they're going to be anyhow." It sounds so simple, yet living by this truth takes a constant practice of letting go. The fact is, *unconditional acceptance and love are the basis for all healing.* Allowing ourselves and others to be as we truly are gives us the space to explore our own potential for change rather than to defend our mistakes, not to mention our choices and preferences. When we acknowledge that we are the way we are, right at this very moment--not exactly the way we'd like to be, but well on the path of growth--then we cease putting our energies into judging ourselves. Instead, we put those energies into creating the kinds of things we'd like to have in our lives.

EXERCISES

1.   Draw a line down the middle of a piece of paper. Make a list on the left side of the criticisms you have had of yourself. (The right side will be used at a later time.)

2.   Draw a line down the middle of another paper. Make a list on the left side of the demands you have made of yourself. (The right side of this will also be used at a later time.)

3.   Go back to any one or more of the Reprogramming Processes you have written. Mark a "C" or a "D" next to each sentence in your mindtalk, indicating which statements were criticisms and which were demands.

4.   List the situations in your life where you are avoiding recognizing that things are the way they are and wanting them to be different. Inventory from the different areas of your life, including relationships, career, family life, love life, finances, spiritual life, intellect, health, appearance, and emotions.

6

The Dynamics Of Choosing To Change

DANCING WITH OUR DEMONS

The past few chapters have discussed how we attempt to create the illusion of self-esteem when we do not have genuine unconditional regard for ourselves. Primarily this is done in two ways. One is perpetuated by our mindtalk, the other by our habits. The first is to live in a cycle of criticisms and demands leveled against ourselves which is supposedly designed to goad us to ever higher levels of performance. If we live up to all these constant perfectionistic demands, an impossible goal, then we may perhaps consider ourselves to be worthwhile. The second is to live in a codependent relationship with a person, pattern or substance, thus relinquishing personal responsibility for our lives.

We may wonder at times why on earth we keep these ridiculous patterns when they clearly do not serve us! We often hang onto our pains and our issues long after we see the mindtalk is false, instead of choosing to change. It is as if there are little invisible demons within us; pulling little strings in our consciousness that make us do things we don't want to do. There is no doubt that it can be frustrating when we stay in old patterns that we know will end up hurting us. Sometimes we do not know where to look for the next step of our growth, for it can be confusing to intellectually know a given behavior can be harmful and yet still feel compelled to continue doing it.

How often have we sworn never to repeat an error again, only to find ourselves once again deeply enmeshed in the old pattern! In fact, there is a whole realm of mindtalk based on how "I should have learned that by now," or, "I should know better than to be upset by this..." Don't buy it; it's just more mindtalk that is not true. *If it were easy to change, we all would have done it long ago.* Beating ourselves up because we wish we could change more quickly *does not* serve us. In fact it slows our path to self-esteem. Looking deeper inside does serve us. When we keep monitoring and noticing our feelings and mindtalk, we can continue to gently chip away at the areas we wish to improve.

Looking at why we keep old patterns is sometimes the hardest part of growth, for it means looking at our hidden motives and reasons. It means facing things we don't want to admit. It means owning up to the real reason for our behaviors instead of the reasons we always tell other people and ourselves. When we face what we don't want to see about ourselves, it can be the most frightening part of our growth. Yet once we face and dance with our "demons", they no longer hold the same power over us. It teaches us humility and gives us a wonderful sense of humor about ourselves.

There are three primary reasons for why we stay stuck in old patterns long after we have seen that they

do not serve us. These are: *habit, comfort,* and, sneaki-
est of all, the *benefits.*

BREAKING OLD HABITS

A habit is something we do because we have "always done it." In psychology it is called a "condi-
tioned response." We light up a cigarette when we're
bored and after a meal. The kids misbehave and we
yell. We feel hurt and we grab a drink. We see someone cry and we say to ourselves "I have to keep my
feelings under control." Or we perceive we are insult-
ed and our mindtalk says, "If I don't tell this person
off, it will mean I'm weak." While some habits are also
physically addictive, the method for breaking a habit
is still the same. *We must first make the decision to
change the habit, then we must do what it takes to change.*

Doing what it takes to change may be somewhat
different for each person, but there are some approaches that consistently prove successful. For example, whatever our habit, it is possible to change it by
ourselves, but it is often much easier if we have a support system. Former First Lady Betty Ford probably
did one of the greatest services anyone ever could
have done for this country by allowing it to be publicly known that she was entering an alcohol rehabilitation program. By choosing to be a role model for
those who were chemically dependent, she in effect
demonstrated that it was not shameful to admit to a
problem and to get support to heal that problem.

It is now considered quite respectable--even ad-
mirable--when we go about getting the support needed to heal ourselves. In addition to the support of our
friends and relatives, there are many support systems,
including the 12-Step or similar lay support programs
(such as Codependents Anonymous, Alcoholics Anonymous, Overeaters Anonymous, Sex and Love Addicts

Anonymous, etc.), psychotherapy, spiritual counseling, group therapy, and the many workshops and classes that are now available.

Changing the physical habits alone, however, is usually insufficient. This is why there is such a high rate of recidivism amongst people who have attempted to break the drug and alcohol habits. *If we do not learn to create good feelings about ourselves through our own self-esteem, the desire to feel better can lead us right back into our old habits in a moment of weakness.* Since all action originates in thought, the *real habit to break is the habit of low self-esteem,* that is, perceiving ourselves as lacking inherent value. In learning the Reprogramming Process, we learned how to be in touch with the demands and criticisms we have placed on ourselves. The more we apply the Reprogramming Process, the more we see how habitual those negative thoughts actually are.

Thought habits are like old rivers. When the waters have run through the same channel for eons, the channel is deep, and there is no reason for the river to change its course. Unless we consciously redirect our mental rivers, our thoughts will continue to run in the same patterns we learned as children when we first cut the riverbed. If we want to rechannel our thinking, we must choose to direct our thoughts down a different course. At first we may forget from time to time that we have a new riverbed, and we will fall into the old habitual interpretations and beliefs without even realizing it. But each time we notice that we have chosen the old river, and consciously redirect our thoughts into the new channel, we reinforce and deepen the new patterns. Gradually the old riverbed dries up.

In order to change our thought habits, we must be willing to nip them at the bud each and every time they arise.

When we catch ourselves in critical mindtalk, we can immediately change it into an acknowledgment. I often used to get up from my desk feeling depressed. I discovered that when this happened, I was usually telling myself I hadn't accomplished enough, even though I had actually worked quite diligently. I simply hadn't fulfilled the unreasonable goals I habitually set for myself. When I noticed this pattern, I began instead to acknowledge myself when I got up from my desk. I would actually do this aloud. "Congratulations, Carolyn," (I'd say to myself), "I'm really proud of you. You've done some wonderful work this morning, and I'm very pleased with the results. Well done!"

EXITING THE COMFORT ZONE

Habit and comfort are related; we stay with old habits because they are comfortable. They may also be painful, but they are familiar, and what is familiar is comfortable. At least we know what to expect. Life is predictable. We know our roles, and our lines are well memorized. Our role may be victim and we may cry every night when our spouse comes home drunk--but it is familiar. Doing something different would not be comfortable. We may rage and punish those around us to the point where they threaten to leave us--but it's what we've always done. Doing something different would be extremely uncomfortable, for we would have to develop a whole new repertoire of attitudes and behaviors. We may keep people at a distance with an act of appearing to be caring when we do not, but since that is what we have always done, it is much more comfortable than facing all the feelings that go with genuine interaction.

Strangely enough, when something is a habit, even when it is painful, we cling to it as if in some way it served us well. In fact, sometimes we actually experience a kind of comfort in wallowing in our pain. It is like an old friend, a favorite old chair, or coffee mug. It is quite similar to watching the soaps. It is regular; it is dependable; it is familiar; it's even a little exciting; and thus it provides a sense of security.

When we step out of our comfort zone, we step out into the unknown. Unless we are a person with great faith, which is not particularly normal for those with low self-esteem, then what is unknown is frightening. We are left with a choice between the pains of our current existence and our fear of who-knows-what. Typically we imagine the unknown to be worse than what we have now, and that can keep us steadfastly bound to our current patterns.

Stepping out of our comfort zone takes courage. When we choose to start doing things differently--by looking at our old behavior patterns, starting into therapy, checking into a rehabilitation program, going to our first 12-Step gathering, or simply beginning to honor ourselves instead of putting ourselves down-- we go out on a limb. We step into the unknown.

Sometimes, however, we wait for life to whack us with a two-by-four before we take that step. Being petitioned for a divorce, getting fired, having an accident--these are the kinds of events that tend to propel us to seek change. The pain forces us out of our comfort zones and we start looking for new ways to live that will not create so much havoc.

Yet we do not need to wait to be forced; the signs of the need for growth are in the little hurts and irritations of our daily lives. Rather than waiting for the painful and traumatic events to catch our attention, we have the option to notice the messages contained in the smaller, daily events. If we pay attention when our spouse says, "Honey, we need to talk," we may never have to hear, "I want a divorce."

By listening to and reprogramming our mindtalk when the small issues come up--even the slightest irritation or hurt--we open new horizons in terms of options and possibilities in our lives. Then, it is up to us to step out into territory that we have never charted before. Whether we choose to step out alone, or grab the hand of someone who has walked that way before, it still takes the courage and the choice to take action.

Learning new mental habits is like learning to ride a bicycle. At first it feels very scary and awkward, and we are a bit wobbly with our new patterns. We may feel foolish and we may even fall sometimes. But like any habit pursued to excellence, in time treating ourselves with genuine self-esteem becomes a natural and comfortable part of living.

THE HIDDEN BENEFITS

As a therapist, I occasionally see people who appear to clear up the same issue over and over again, but never seem to apply it to their lives. There is a sense of being stuck, of almost not wanting to change. In situations like this, there is usually some kind of *benefit* or *payoff*--sometimes called *secondary gains*--that we get from keeping the painful situation or the old habits (Cormier & Cormier, 1985). While this may not seem logical, it is actually quite common that we will retain harmful behavior because the alternatives appear to be too frightening. Although it is not always readily apparent, we often actually keep the current or old behavior because there is something we get from it. We *want* the benefits of the old beliefs and habits *more* than we want the newer, more healthy behaviors and perspectives.

Some years ago, there were two women associates whom I greatly resented. While I worked with them in two totally different capacities, they were both in positions of greater authority than myself. They were both very powerful and doing the kind of spiritual and psychological work that I wanted to do. I judged them both as being very domineering and believed they somehow were keeping me from truly fulfilling my own work. I perhaps would have written the problem off as the other person's authoritarianism if there had not been two of them, but since the dynamic was the same in two separate areas of my life, it caught my attention. I looked to see my own role in perpetuating the situation.

Having reprogrammed my mindtalk a number of times without moving any closer to releasing my resentments, I decided to look at the benefits. What was I getting by maintaining my resentments against these women? What did I get to do or not do; how did I get to see myself; what did those resentments give me permission to do or not to do (Brown and Whitten, 1983)? I discovered that my resentments gave me permission to see myself as the victim of these two women. I got to see myself as well-intentioned and long-suffering, and I blamed *them* for keeping me from doing the work of which I'd always dreamed. My mindtalk permitted me to use that resentment to stay safely in the victim role and thus avoid risking and stepping out to fulfill my dreams. I was making them responsible for me. In continuing to work under them and in their systems, I was avoiding stepping into my own power and creating my own system.

When it finally became clear that I had wanted the benefits of safety and comfort more than I wanted to take responsibility for my long cherished vision, I decided that those benefits were not worth it. I decided I didn't need to be long-suffering and well-intentioned to be a good person, and that the stretch of risking and being a little uncomfortable was worth seeing my dreams come true. As I began to powerfully produce the results I wanted in my life, I no longer needed resentments of someone else's power to give me permission--and the excuse--to hold back on my own power. By giving up those dubious "benefits", I took control over my own life.

Sometimes we remain "stuck" in a certain issue, with certain problems that never seem to change, or with a given behavior that we keep saying we want to change but never do. Norm had said that he wanted to work less hours and spend time with his family, but that it simply wasn't possible. Even though over the years he had had three different jobs, he typically retained a pattern of working a sixty hour week.

When Norm looked deeper he discovered that his workaholic habits gave him the benefit of an excuse to avoid intimacy with his wife and children while he projected the image of a hard-working provider. He had an even greater benefit of being too busy to face or deal with his own low self-esteem issues, and therefore had a reason not to grow or change. It was not until his wife had an affair that he decided there were things in his own personality and his marriage on which he wanted to work.

People often say, "Well, I really want to change, but I just can't." However, if we convert that sentence to, "Part of me would really like to change, but there is a greater part that chooses not to," we generally have a more accurate sentence. This is not surprising if we give it some thought. When we are faced with two conflicting things that we want, we choose the one we want most. Often what we choose is simply to be comfortable and secure rather than choosing to risk change. In other words, the hidden benefits of staying the same often have more appeal to us than the risky and unknown benefits of change.

Janet was in one of my Self-Esteem classes. She believed that her family was forcing her to use her money in ways she did not wish to. She believed they were responsible for her choices. She had learned the Reprogramming Process, but when it came time to re-program her mindtalk, she persisted in the position that all of her negative mindtalk was true. She did not want to step into her "Higher Power" perspective and see what was very obvious to the rest of the class-- that she had the power to make her own decisions about her money. This was part of a conversation in which she discovered the benefits of not telling her-self the truth about her inherent value:

Janet: I was real disappointed when it came to the part of the Reprogramming Process about telling the truth; I couldn't do that, or even objectively look at it.

CB: Let's see what the benefit might be of hold-ing on to your old programs. Try saying this state-ment: "I don't want to move into my Higher Power."

Janet: (with the sound of a whine in her voice) I don't like the way that sounds.

CB: I'm sure it's not comfortable for you, but let's see what happens.

Janet: I don't want to move into my power.

CB: ...because if I do...

Janet: ...because if I do, I'll have to let go beating myself up.

CB: And if you let go of beating yourself up-- then what will you have to do?

Janet: I'll have to... (pauses, then smiles) give up wanting others to take care of me and start taking care of myself.

CB: Did you get taken care of when you were

little?

Janet: No. I didn't get much love.

CB: Probably not as much as you wanted. You see, when we beat ourselves up a lot, then we want other people to save and take care of us. That way we stay in the codependent cycle. We can never be happy or satisfied because we are trying to get other people to give us self-esteem, which of course is impossible. SELF-esteem is when *we* honor our own *self*.

Only when we take care of ourselves first can we eliminate the false notion that others can make us happy. By avoiding the truth of our inherent self-worth, we have the benefit of maintaining the illusion that, as in the case of Janet, we can get others to love us and take care of us and we resent feeling powerless. Unfortunately, it doesn't work, for the others resent being inappropriately responsible for us. The benefits are the reasons why we stay in our old patterns, but the benefits are as much an illusion as the other untrue mindtalk we tell ourselves.

Again, it is like the mouse on the treadmill. It feels as if we are accomplishing something, but we are not. We are recycling the same patterns, when the door out of the cage--the truth of our own self-worth-- is right there standing open. The hidden benefits give us an excuse or reason to stay in the cage--in the comfort zone. *The ultimate benefit for not claiming our self-esteem is the avoidance of taking responsibility for our lives.* However, there are many variations on this basic benefit, depending on the values with which we grew up and our own personal *modus operandi*.

Here are some favorite hidden benefits which help to give us an excuse for not changing our old patterns. Some are well disguised as looking virtuous, but when they are used to avoid the truth, we can know for sure that they will bind us in low self-esteem. In order to discover what benefits we are getting by retaining old codependent patterns, we can ask ourselves what those patterns give us permission to a) do or not do, or b) see ourselves as. For the sake of convenience, these benefits are divided according to the typical codependency styles, but clearly we each have our own personal combination.

If I'm a CARETAKER type of codependent, my hidden benefits to staying in old habits and beliefs may be to:
> See myself as a good person, holy, virtuous, cheerful and nice
> See myself as the responsible one
> See myself as victim and martyr
> See myself as long-suffering, hard working, sacrificing, and helpful
> Have permission to be involved in others' affairs
> Have permission to show anger and insults disguised with a smile
> Have permission to indulge in food, shopping, resting, and other things to make up for all I have done for others
> Have permission to let others take responsibility for me
> Have permission to control others
> Have permission to avoid looking at my own issues and behavior

If I'm a DOMINATING type of codependent, my hidden benefits to staying in old habits and beliefs may be to:
> See myself as powerful, in charge, strong, and effective

See myself as the responsible one
See myself as right
Have permission to make sure I get my way
Have permission to avoid vulnerability
Have permission to rage or ignore others'
    feelings
Have permission to hide in work, alcohol, sexual
    encounters, etc.
Have permission to control others
Have permission to avoid looking at my own
    issues and behavior

If I'm a MANIPULATING type of codependent,
my hidden benefits to staying in old habits and beliefs
may be to:
See myself as the one who can keep things
    organized
See myself as having the correct view and the
    right answers to problems
See myself as the responsible one
Have permission to see others' perspective and
    feelings as invalid and thus ignore them
Have permission to get what I want no matter
    what
Have permission to withhold love and affection
Have permission to avoid intimacy
Have permission to control others
Have permission to avoid looking at my own
    issues and behavior

If I'm an AVOIDING type of codependent, my
hidden benefits to staying in old habits and patterns
may be to:
See myself as controlled, calm, and unemotional
See myself as independent, self-sufficient
See myself as being above conflict

See myself as victim

Have permission to avoid facing problems

Have permission to be passive-aggressive (ie,
   withhold what another wants, or give them
   what they don't want)

Have permission to make others responsible
   for me

Have permission to withhold love and avoid
   intimacy

Have permission to control others

Have permission to avoid looking at my own
   issues and behavior

Benefits are often subconscious. It is not easy for us to acknowledge that we have a deep need to be right, or to avoid intimacy, or to rage, or be passive-aggressive. This is the type of benefit we do not like to admit to ourselves, much less to others. Yet when we have a belief that we "should" or "have to" be a certain way--in control, cheerful, powerful--and we are afraid that we cannot measure up to that demand, then we attempt to create the illusion that we are those things in order to be able to perceive ourselves as worthy. Once we claim our true self-esteem, we accept ourselves the way we are. We can say to ourselves, "Well, sometimes I get out of control," or "Sometimes I can really be grouchy or act afraid"--and we know we're still worthwhile. We no longer need the convoluted structure of criticisms and demands along with codependent behavior to maintain appearances. *Being imperfect IS acceptable.*

THE PRICE WE PAID

Even though we got the "benefit" of the illusion of worth from the lies our minds told us, we also paid an enormous price for maintaining those illusions. We made compromises in every area of our lives in order to keep the drama going, but above all, we gave up the most important things we have. We paid the price of our integrity, our feelings, our freedom. *We sold out the most important person in our lives: our self.*

It is when we look at the cost of our negative patterns that we are able to realize that the benefits are not worthwhile. If we give consideration to each of the different areas of our lives, we can see how much we have paid to stay in our cages. Here is a list created by one Self-Esteem workshop of what it cost them to maintain codependent behaviors and negative beliefs about themselves:

> Living with anxiety, depression, fear, anger, hurt, guilt, resentment, and other negative emotions
>
> Low self-esteem
>   Don't know what I want, can't make decisions
>   Think I'm a failure so I don't even try
>   Blaming and criticizing myself
>   No self-respect
>
> Physical results of those "stuffed" feelings, including
>   Chronic backache
>   Migraines, headaches
>   Colitis, ulcers, and digestive disorders
>   Hunched over, poor posture
>   Aging lines that show worry and anger
>   Obesity
>   High medical costs
>
> Unsatisfying relationships
>   Divorce, or many short relationships
>   Lack of integrity, honesty about myself

Lack of intimacy, sharing
Lack of communication
Constant fighting
Separation, isolation, loneliness
Feeling numb, out of touch with me and others
Passing on dysfunctional systems to our
    children

Addictions
    Codependency
    Alcoholism and drug abuse
    Our children learn from us to choose addiction
    Smoking
    Money wasted on compulsive spending,
        gambling, eating, alchohol, drugs, etc.
    Time wasted in fantasy, TV, hiding from life

Career problems
    Never tried to reach goals
    Getting fired
    Low income
    Unfulfilled dreams
    Choose unfulfilling work
    Workaholic

Living in a spiritual vacuum
    Don't think God cares about me
    Using religion to perpetuate negative feelings
        rather than source of inspiration
    No faith or experience of spiritual life

Energy level low
    Feel bored
    Feel tired from trying so hard
    Don't do things I enjoy
    Don't enjoy things I do

Sometimes we are so used to life as we have always lived it that we do not see the price we pay. Yet looking at the cost can have the powerful effect of catapulting us into the resolve to step out of old patterns and start being all that we are capable of being. When we look at the cost, it becomes apparent that the benefits simply are not worth it. From here on it becomes evident that the only choice that makes sense in our lives is to undertake with dedication--and patience--to heal ourselves. If we have the energy and will to create codependency with our thoughts, then we also have the power to create the dynamic and fulfilling lifestyle that is available when we claim our self-esteem.

EXERCISES

1.   On the left side of a new page, list all the old patterns which you have wanted to change but have not. Then, on the right side indicate whether you have maintained those behaviors because of habit, comfort, a particular set of benefits, or any combination of those three.

2.   Go back to the exercises in Chapter two. List the benefits you have gained from a) the things you have called yourself, and b) your "shoulds," "shouldn'ts," "have to's," "can'ts," "nevers" and "alwayses." Next go to the Reprogramming Processes you did in Chapter Three and since then, and list the benefits that your negative mindtalk provided for you. When you have completed it, go back to the lists in this chapter and compare; see if there are some items you might have forgotten.

3.   Next, for all of the above benefits, also list the price you paid for each. What patterns do you see?

4.   Consider each of the benefits you have listed and decide if they are worth maintaining. For those that are, take full responsibility for your choice and be at peace in that choice. For those that are not, list the steps you plan to take to make the changes you want. Review these steps after reading the final chapters and see if you would like to add anything.

7

The Higher Self:
Being All
That We Can Be

WE ARE OUR OWN ANSWERS

In addition to my Self-Esteem workshop, I also teach a weekend meditation intensive. It is always held in a very beautiful country environment, perfect for searching out the depths of our hearts and minds, for silent walks, and for sharing with others on their own paths of growth. One of the things we do that weekend is to each read a paragraph or passage from some book that has been an inspiration for us, and to talk about how it has impacted us personally. Joan, a public school resource teacher, shared the following from *Advice From a Failure*, by Jo Coudert (1965).

"You do not need to be loved, not at the cost of yourself! The single relationship that is truly central and crucial in a life is the relationship to the self. It is rewarding to find someone...you like, but it is essential to like yourself. It is quickening to recognize that someone is a good and decent human being, but it is indispensable to view yourself as acceptable. It is a delight to discover people who are worthy of respect, admiration and love, but it is vital to believe yourself deserving of these things.

"For you cannot live in someone else. You cannot find yourself in someone else. Of all the people you will know in a lifetime, you are the only one you will never leave nor lose. To the question of your life, you are the only answer. To the problems of your life, you are the only solutions" (p. 131).

These two paragraphs delightfully and powerfully summarize the essence of this book. Until now we have looked at the questions and problems of our lives; our next step is to address the answers and solutions.

Identifying what hasn't worked is the first step to fixing it. This is why we have, so far, focused on the beliefs and habits that have perpetuated low self-esteem. When the light goes on in the dashboard of our car, do we open the hood and start unscrewing every nut and bolt we can see? Do we change the tire because that's the only thing we know how to do? Not at all. We listen and watch carefully; we test a few things here and there. We bring in an expert or get a book about the problem if we don't have enough data to determine what we need to do. Thus, in order to rid ourselves of the "warning lights"--the painful situations in our lives--we start by identifying what hurts and why.

Finally, once we know what needs to be fixed, whether it is our codependency or our carburetor, we must take the steps necessary to make repairs. Of course we could just run the vehicle into the ground, shortening its lifespan and lessening the quality of service we get from it in the meantime. Many people do this with their lives. Or we can walk a path of learning, of growth, of expansion. The choice is up to us each and every moment of each and every day. Let it go, or do something about it.

We are the answers and solutions to our lives because we make the choice whether to grow or to stay the same. It is no one else's job to make us feel good; we alone can take responsibility to make that happen. We are also the answers and solutions because all the information we need for our transformation lies within ourselves. If we choose to opt for maximum service from our vehicle, we do not look under someone else's hood to see why ours doesn't work, nor do we replace their carburetor when ours needs adjustment. Yet ironically, this is what we most often do with our personal lives.

When I first got divorced, I dated a man who was sometimes very nice, but sometimes also abusive. I talked to a therapist friend of mine, complaining about his behavior and wondering what I could do about it (ie., about *his* carburetor). She looked at me and shrugged, "I don't know why you think you need to do something about him; it's *your* issue." "*My issue?*" I was shocked. "How can it be *my* issue; he's the one being obnoxious." "Yes," she answered, "and you're the one choosing to hang out with someone who does not treat you well."

Gulp. It took me a while to acknowledge that what she had said was true. I was getting plenty of benefits from seeing myself as the good and caring victim, and at the same time avoiding being alone. But she was right; it wasn't his carburetor, it was my own choice of fuel. Years later I discovered that my poor choice of fuel was my low self-esteem, but the important lesson I learned at that time was, when I don't like what's going on in my life, look to myself. After years of trying to get the other person to be different so I could be comfortable, I finally began working on what only I could change--myself.

HONORING THE SELF

When we have finally acknowledged that our codependent patterns don't work, then revved up our courage and determination to do something about it, we need to find specific ways to go about creating the change that we want in our lives. Anyone who has ever repaired a car knows that once we have decided what needs fixing, we must make sure we have the correct tools to do the job. Otherwise the job may take twice as long and never be done quite right--a makeshift patch job, not fine craftsmanship.

How do we know what tools to use? We generally apply a combination of what seems reasonable and what feels right--logic and intuition. Then, with experience, we come to know what works best for us. This book contains many such tools which can effect profound growth. These exercises work when we use them. We will each have certain ones that work better for us than others. Sometimes we will make up our own variations or new exercises. It doesn't take a degree in psychology to think up some good ways to expand our horizons. Be creative. Remember, we are the answers and solutions to our own lives.

Sometimes we are lucky enough--or should we say, creative enough--to find assistance on our path. Certain books may be very useful in addressing our needs; or we may find a support group, such as one of the 12-Step Programs. We may augment our own personal work with the input of a therapist or counselor, someone who is trained and skilled, and has the ability to facilitate our growth. All these are important, yet we must remember that *we* are still responsible for our own path and our own choices. Even the "experts" are people, and no person is more of an expert about us than we are ourselves. It doesn't matter who thinks what about who we are or what we should do. We are constantly surrounded by other people's opinions--those of our spouse, our friends, our boss, our kids, our church, and our therapist. But ultimately, we must check our choices against our own system of beliefs and values. We are the answers and the solutions to our own lives.

When I first graduated from college, I moved to New York City. There I met an expert who told me I needed a psychotherapist. I asked several experts who I should see and was finally referred to a woman who was reputed to be, of course, quite an expert. I sat in front of her each week, staring down at her elaborate Persian carpet, talking about the problems of my life. A year passed, and she told me she would be going on vacation, and wanted to address any issues that existed between the two of us. She thought maybe there were some things I didn't like about my work with her. I was surprised; it had never occurred to me to question the nature of our interaction. I assured her there were no problems, and agreed to call her to make an appointment when she returned.

But, I went home and thought about it. I really didn't like her a bit. In fact, I never had. She sat in a giant expensive black leather chair with her feet up on a huge leather ottoman a short distance from my face. Her sofa--my place to sit--was about four inches lower than her chair, so she always towered over me. Aside from sitting surrounded by black, she almost always wore black. She never smiled that I can remember, and the cold expression on her face never changed, no matter what I was saying. I realized that was why I spent so much time mentally tracing the intricate patterns of her carpet. I then received perhaps the most important insight of my year with her: If I didn't like her, she wasn't the right therapist for me. I found another therapist of whom I was very fond-- and whom I admired for her skill as a therapist as well. Three months of work with her, and my life had new direction and purpose.

I often recommend that my clients attend a 12-Step Program. Janie went to a Codependents Anonymous (CODA) Program for three months, but wasn't happy with the program. Finally she told me about it. "The people in my group are all professionals; as a mother alone at home with three kids, I don't relate to what they talk about. It's as if they have one kind of codependency and I have another." "What would feel more appropriate for you?" I asked. She said she'd like to be in a group of people who were more in alignment with her lifestyle. "Well, go for it!" I said, "Honor you inner promptings."

Janie had felt the need to attend a different group from the time she first started, but because her mind-talk said that her group and her therapist were the experts, she did not follow what felt right for her. As soon as she recognized that she had turned her power over to others, she took the matter into her own hands. Although she had to drive a little further to meetings, she was happy to find a CODA group which was much more focused on the family issues which were relevant to her.

Probably the most important shift in perspective that we can make when starting to heal our lives, is to stop believing that the answers to our problems are "out there." As John Bradshaw explains in *The Family* (1988), the sense of our own being is only gained when we develop our own inner life. Unfortunately, few of us received the kind of education that taught us to use our internal resources. While education in our country is very sophisticated in a technological sense, it is still very primitive in terms of teaching our children living and coping skills. We still go to school to be "filled" with knowledge from teachers and books; rarely do we run into that unique kind of teacher who helps us learn to delight in our own natural process of discovery, who helps us to uncover the wisdom and understanding that already exist within each of us.

In the Native American Indian culture, the children and the eldest members of the community are honored as the ones with wisdom. As children we are naturally honest and intuitively wise--until we become filled with negative beliefs about ourselves and lose confidence in our intuition. Much of our work on ourselves is to once again, "become as little children", to regain that natural connection and honesty with ourselves that children have.

I was sitting with some children at a picnic not long ago. Matt came over and asked Joey to go play ball with him. "No, I think I want to sit here and read," Joey said, "maybe later." "OK," shrugged Matt, and off he ran to find another playmate. I was fascinated--neither child tried to manipulate or be dishonest with the other. Neither seemed to have mindtalk or negative thoughts about himself or his friend. Each child was clear about his own desires and choices, but honored his friend's perspective.

How often will we as adults be that true to ourselves? There was a time that it would not have occurred to me to tell a friend that I didn't want to go out because I was going to read! I would think I needed a better excuse--like being sick or having to work. I would tell a little lie, then feel guilty while I sat there trying to read. Today I am much more comfortable with following what feels right for me, and with being honest about it. That kind of clarity feels better for me and for my friends as well.

As we learn to let go of the lies we have told our-
selves--that we "should keep our feelings to ourselves," or that we "have to do what other people
want so they will love us"--we gradually begin to be
honest about who we are, what we feel, and what we
want. It ceases to make sense that we would do anything but live in complete alignment with ourselves.
When we pretend to feel or look like something we
are not, we live in a precarious balance attempting to
keep that illusion in place. When we put *being ourselves* before "looking good," we may find that some of
the people who were attracted to that false self disappear from our lives, *but* whole new horizons open
where we can relax into a lifestyle in which we do
what feels right for us, and where we spend time with
those who are naturally in alignment with us.

At first, being completely honest is very scary
and risky, since we have so long believed that our
personal value was conditional upon what we pro-
duced and who we kept happy. As we begin to think
of ourselves as unconditionally worthy, it may seem
as if we are in a no-man's-land; it's as if we need to
hook our self-esteem to something, and we're not sure
what that might be. Gradually it becomes clear that
*SELF-esteem is esteem generated from the inside, that no
one else and nothing else can give that worth to us,* save
the perceptual shift within our own minds that says:
"I'm just great, right the way I am."

Emily had a very codependent relationship with
her mother. For years her mother had made many of
Emily's decisions for her. She helped Emily shop for
clothes, gave approval of all of her living arrange-
ments, and was extremely involved in her career
choices. When Emily first came to therapy, she did
not know where she stopped and her mother began.

As she started defining her own boundaries and making her own choices, her mother reacted with anger
and hurt, complaining to Emily that she no longer felt
useful.

At first Emily felt very guilty. Then she reacted
by shutting her mother out of everything in order to
regain a sense of herself. Later, as she learned to be
very clear with her mother as to what her own decisions and preferences were, her mother gradually
found other things to do to feel useful, and they re-
established the closeness they once had, but this time
Emily functioned from appropriate boundaries and a
sense of self-esteem.

Honoring ourselves does not mean we need to
dishonor anyone else. Nor does it mean we need to
stop being loving and helpful to others. It does, however, mean that we cease giving and serving when we
are solely motivated by gaining approval. It also
means we stop doing for others when we need to turn
our attention to our own needs. In other words, we
take responsibility for ourselves. That way our giving
and our receiving come into balance.

BEING HUMAN BEINGS

As we practice honoring and respecting our-
selves--both when we shine and when we act like
fools--we gradually let go of looking outside to find
mirrors of our value. We recognize that the only
measuring stick that matters is our own. We start developing ourselves as our own resource. We develop
ways of checking inside ourselves when we make decisions. When we feel uncomfortable, we learn to listen to the discomfort and see what it is telling us. We
begin to honor our intuition--the tiny voices inside
that say "Yes, do that," and "No, don't do that"--*before*
they become the thundering mindtalk that says, "I

should have known better."

As we become more grounded in genuine self-esteem, we cease to make excuses for our preferences and for our errors. In other words, if we have unconditional self-regard, then we see our preferences, desires and choices as equally valid as anyone else's. We tend to let go of concerns for who is right and who is wrong, and allow for--even applaud--our human differences.

As we become established in our self-esteem, we recognize and accept that we make mistakes. We no longer see errors as cause for a string of self-abusive mindtalk, but instead, use those errors as ways to learn how to do things better. We stop *criticizing* ourselves as inadequate and *demanding* of ourselves that we be perfect. We can let go of that illusory control over ourselves and others and acknowledge that we do not have to be perfect; *we are humans.* Or, we might say, we are perfect humans. We are not supposed to be at our goal already; we are, *appropriately,* on a path of evolution.

Let's face it, if we were at that point of perfection already, on that mountaintop to which we have all long aspired, we would simply see another mountain that would be quite interesting to climb. When I was a little girl (and frankly, well into my adulthood), I really did think that after Prince Charming kissed me, it was "happily ever after, THE END." I didn't understand that life continues on with its daily ups and downs, that reaching one goal was the beginning of another. I would always subvert my efforts to reach my goals because I simply could not conceive of what would happen on the other side of the mountain--once I reached my goal.

Now I know life is a never-ending process of exploring and expanding. Our different goals are simply markers along the road, not the end of the story. When we have self-esteem, we recognize that making mistakes is perhaps our greatest resource for progress and growth, for it shows us what doesn't work. That way we are closer to knowing what *does* work. We become more tolerant and patient with our own weaknesses. We actually begin to love ourselves unconditionally, to treat ourselves with respect, to do unto ourselves with the same kindness we usually are willing to do unto others. And, as we find ourselves acceptable, both when we have done well and when we haven't, we automatically develop understanding and compassion for others' shortcomings.

There is a wonderful and wise science fiction book called *2150, A.D.*, by Thea Alexander (1971). The main character is a student who is catapulted in his dreams from his college dorm to a progressive future society. This society does not believe in failure, *per se.* Instead, they believe that it takes a certain number of failures to reach any given success. Each error is a part of the process of becoming successful. Therefore, every mistake is applauded, for it is considered a "success-failure." So if a given goal takes twenty-one tries, and you have just had success-failure number seventeen, everyone is happy for you because you are progressing to your goal. Adopting this perspective is a great boon to our self-esteem, for in truth, errors *are* stepping stones to success.

When we honor ourselves unconditionally, rather than being disgusted or depressed by things that don't go well, we become curious, interested, awakened to the idea that we have discovered something new to add to our lives. We begin to see our mistakes as gifts, as the blessings in diguise which give us the key to a new and better way of life. In Chapter One I shared the stories of two major events that absolutely rocked the foundations of my life. Those experiences were completely devastating. They were the most painful experiences I could imagine.

Today I look back on those unpleasant events with enormous gratitude. They forced me to look inside and make the changes I needed to be as happy as I am today. I wouldn't trade those experiences for anything in this world--and I mean that literally. When we honor our hurt, our anger, our mistakes, and our personal preferences--as well as all the good and easy stuff--we bring to light an enormous amount of information for living our lives creatively and in alignment with ourselves. We ourselves become an exciting discovery. We are a new book, and each day is another page where new adventures are unraveled.

THE HIGHER SELF

Each of us has had times in our lives when we drew on resources we did not know we had. We have all at some time experienced finding an extra burst of speed to win a race when we thought there was not another ounce of energy left. Or perhaps we have been surprised to hear ourselves speak insightful words from a source of wisdom we didn't realize that we had. Or we have discovered we were right when we had a premonition or when we chose a course of action, not based on logic, but simply because it felt right.

When I was in high school, I wanted very much to be a cheerleader. During tryouts we each had to do a routine that included doing a cartwheel ending up in the splits. Now, I could *not* do the splits. I had given up ballet as a child because I was embarassingly inflexible. It was out of the question. But I wanted to be a cheerleader *badly*. So I went ahead and learned the routine and signed up for tryouts. As I stood before the judges, all of a sudden all the butterflies in my stomach disappeared and I became very calm. I put on a brilliant demonstration, completing with an elegant cartwheel landing perfectly in the splits. I remember feeling the shock of seeing my body in a position it had never been in--and never has since. I bounced back to my feet and ran clapping appropriately off the stage, amazed. I not only made cheerleading, but I was elected captain. (And fortunately we were able to design plenty of excellent routines that did not ever require me to repeat that performance.)

It is said that we only use about a tenth of our brains. We have all heard dramatic stories of people who have somehow tapped into "superhuman" abilities--a grandmother who lifts a car off of an injured child, a skier who manages to stay alive trapped for days under an avalanche, a man who places his hand over a wound and discovers he has stopped the bleeding. Countless such events are scientifically documented. We are fascinated by examples of the human potential. But we tend to tuck these experiences away in our mental files under "Curiosities" or, "Possible for others, but not for me"--and forget about them. We ignore the enormous implications such experiences have. Because our belief systems do not acknowledge such potential, we complacently settle for less.

We are all powerfully creative beings. We can all be much, much more if we choose to be. All it takes is a shift in our thoughts. Remember, our thoughts are the creative force of our lives. If our thoughts are centered around self-criticism and seeing what we are not, we create our lives in alignment with those thoughts. If we see ourselves as magnificent, delightful, loving, kind, and worthy of many good things, that is what we create. As we start to understand the magnitude of the power of our thoughts, we then recognize that our only option is to take resonsibility for what goes on in our minds each and every moment, no matter how abusive or sad our lives may have been before. It is up to *each* of us to leap out of our own darkness and step into the light.

I once saw a painting that had a whole row of people lined up on the bottom of the canvas. There was one person above the others, apparently relaxing in the air. A wavey line led from the row of people below to the top where she was floating. Underneath, there was a caption that read, "One day, fed up with hell, she simply upped and left." Sometimes we get into thinking that we are bound by our past, but we are not. Man is a creature of habit unless he applies his will, and chooses to live by the power of his choice rather than the force of habit. We do have free will--*if* we use it. We can all live in exactly the way we have always dreamed if we learn to use the creative powers of our minds.

We all have our good sides and our bad sides. I do, you do, the derelict who hangs out on the corner does, and so does the President of the United States. But where do we focus our attention? Do we constantly focus on our mistakes and shortcomings, berating ourselves and feeling depressed because we are so lousy? Or do we glean any important information from each mistake and turn our attention with enthusiasm back to whatever we have chosen to create in our lives? Where do we put our focus? Do we focus on what we don't like about ourselves or do we focus on the really neat and interesting things that we love? The choice is ours. It's like the proverbial question, "Is your glass half empty or half full?" It is not appropriate to ignore the areas where we still need to learn and grow, but neither do we have to be consumed by them. We can choose to move *towards* what we love, what fascinates, delights and nourishes us. We can focus on our lives from the perspective of our Higher Self.

Our Higher Self is that greater part of us from which we sometimes draw in times of deep inner focus, exhilaration, or extreme crisis. It is that part we use when we tap in to our intuition, our wisdom, and those abilities that seem to be beyond what we think of as normal. In daily life, we often fall into identifying with our own struggles and our weaknesses; we are at these times seeing ourselves as no more than our personalities.

However, *who we REALLY are is something greater*. We all have parts of ourselves that operate for our growth and expansion beyond those functions of which we are aware in our normal conscious mind. These parts have been variously identified as our subconscious, superconscious, dreamstate, intuition, our observer state, and our Higher Self. As we quiet the mindtalk, that distracting and self-deprecating internal chatter, we begin to operate from the perspective of our greater potential, our Higher Self. Gradually, through the different methods of processing our inner struggles and honoring who we are, we develop the ability to see and live our lives in the confidence and peace that is the perspective of our own Higher Self.

OUR HIGHER POWER

If our Higher Self is the connection to our greater potential, then our Higher Power is our connection to God. At times, when we are centered and clear, it may be difficult to distinguish between the two, for our greatest experience of God occurs within our own selves. Bradshaw (1988) explains that the movement towards a knowledge of ourselves *is* a journey towards Spirituality. Perhaps because long ago we separated our culture in terms of church and state, we often disengage our psychological processes from our spiritual life. Mental and emotional well-being got assigned to the secular quarter, separate from the spiritual, and the twain rarely meet.

One of the few exceptions to this has been Alcoholics Anonymous and the other 12-Step Programs. While dealing with addictions and related psychological problems, the 12-Step approach is primarily spiritual. Somewhat paraphrasing the first three steps of these programs, they include, 1) recognizing the unmanageability of our codependency or addiction, 2) acknowledging that a Power greater than ourselves can restore balance to our lives, and 3) making the decision to turn our will and our lives over to the care of our Higher Power, or God as we understand Him. It is a premise of this enormously effective program that it is through spiritual emphasis that we begin to get clarity in our lives (Friends in Recovery, 1987).

These and the remaining nine steps do not attempt to convert a person to a particular belief system; they are principles which are common to all religions. I believe they also contain the essential elements of any physical, emotional or mental healing process. What is extremely significant here is that the 12-Step Programs, without any financial backing or organizational administration, have become the single greatest movement for psychological change in the country. And they are, at their core, spiritual in nature. What this says to me is that *we cannot ignore our spiritual component when we are working to heal our lives.* It does not matter what our religion is. What matters is that in our healing, we acknowledge and invite the help of God, however we happen to interpret or conceive of Him/Her/It.

For most of us growing up, God was an elusive grandfather figure who lived somewhere in the sky over the house where we lived. If we were raised in a religious family, we may have been taught to be as good as possible in order to win His favor and to petition in prayer for His help when in need. Usually, however, little instruction was given in how to hear if our requests were answered in any form. If our early lives were spent in a non-religious family, one of the reasons for the lack of a Higher Power in our lives was simply that there was a lack of evidence that It existed. Either way, God often remained intangible, somewhat uncommunicative, and sometimes painfully absent when we were most needy.

How can we establish a real and tangible relationship with God, however we may perceive Him to exist? The first step is to recognize that we ourselves limit God, who is in essence *limitless*. So often we try to define what God is, but in truth, this is impossible. It matters not what our religious affiliation; all religions acknowledge that God is everywhere, existing in all things, that He is all powerful, that He is all seeing, that there is nowhere that God is not. Because our *minds* are limited, this is not something we can readily understand. Our only access to true comprehension of this limitlessness is through the direct experience which occurs when we silence our minds.

What this immediately tells us is that, among other places that God exists, He also exists within each of us. This is a concept with which many of us are already familiar, at least on an intellectual level. More often than not, however, we have been trained to seek God outside ourselves. As with many things in our society, we pray to or meditate on an external

God who will somehow send us answers, guidance, or peace from "beyond". We rely on priests, rabbis, psychics, spiritual books, or any one of thousands of possible sources other than ourselves in order to create our connection with God. We may think of Him as too "busy" to deal with our little problems. We may even think of God in the same codependent manner we see other relationships. But these ideas limit That which has no limits.

If God is in all things, then this external means of finding God has, of course, a certain amount of validity. Yet if God is also within each of us, then there can be no outside source more valid, more meaningful, and more personally appropriate than the relationship we develop with God within our own selves. It is the acknowledgment and reliance on God within that becomes our greatest Resource. When we perceive of ourselves as worthwhile, we open ourselves to receiving the grace and the help that God offers.

There are a number of ways of magnifying and increasing our relationship with the God Within. Prayer, of course, is one such means of our connection with God. By becoming very quiet inside and placing what is in our hearts on the altar, so to speak, we invite in and open ourselves to assistance from our Higher Power. Answers may come to us in meditation or prayer as we still our mindtalk and dive into the silence.

Or God, as we conceive of Him, may answer by connecting us with certain people or events that are needed in our lives. For example, if we have asked for patience, we need to be aware that the next clumsy or slow person who comes into our life is not an irritant, but an opportunity to practice patience. Life is God speaking to us in every moment; if we are attuned to the God within, we say "yes" to our trials, and we grow in peace. If we say "no," attempting to control situations and people which we have no business controlling, we miss the gifts given by Our Higher Power.

MEDITATION

One of the most powerful ways to create a connection with ourselves, our own feelings and thoughts, our Higher Self, and our experience of God, is meditation. As we practice silencing our minds, we begin to eliminate the one thing that keeps us limited and thus separate from a limitless God: our thoughts. As we enter into the silence within, we open ourselves to receiving the peace and the guidance that is there for us.

The God Within speaks through our bodies as well as through our silenced minds. When the mind-talk is stilled, we learn to pay attention to responses our bodies make. When faced with a decision or choice, it is possible to notice the body's reaction, especially in the area of the heart. Does it expand, feel relaxed and move toward a goal, or does it feel contracted, tight, and withdrawing? Do we breathe easier or stop breathing? As we honor this wonderful barometer for our intuition, our connectedness with ourselves and the God Within grows.

Meditation has an added benefit: While we are practicing but have not yet achieved a silent mind (which, indeed, is not an overnight process), we can come to know our thoughts on an intimate level. We can become aware of the emotional and mental habits and patterns that keep us busy and distracted, and hence disconnected from our Higher Self and our Higher Power. As we become familiar with our "favorite" ways of keeping ourselves separate from our own inner connection, then we can apply the various tools and processes for clearing those habits and patterns.

The internal resources for growth are much more accessible for people who meditate than in those individuals who do not spend that daily time with themselves. We might liken the mind to a large glass holding both water and oil. The water is our subconscious thoughts which lie on the bottom of the glass. Looking down into the glass, we are not aware of them. The oil is our conscious thoughts, floating on the surface and much more discernible. When we do not meditate, we remain relatively oblivious to the greater portion of our own thoughts. When we meditate, it is as if we are increasing the proportion of oil to water. It helps us to know ourselves better, to relax, to control our thoughts better, and it consequently improves whatever form of work we are doing on ourselves.

The steps to practicing meditation are simple. Set aside a specific time and place to meditate each day. When there is regularity, the mind settles into meditation more easily. Make a commitment as to how long the meditation period will be. A half hour is a good amount of time, although twenty, fifteen, or even five minutes will give excellent results. Building up to forty-five minutes or longer will be very beneficial for those who are very committed to meditating.

Sit in a comfortable position with the spine straight. Now become aware of the breath. Notice the inhalation, then the point in which the inhalation becomes an exhalation, then notice the exhalation, then the point where the exhalation becomes the inhalation. Just watch, letting the breathing be relaxed.

For those who prefer a little more involvement to help sustain the meditation, it is possible to focus the mind on either the heart or the point between the eyebrows. It is also helpful to use an affirmation or *mantra* to which the mind returns each time it wanders. "I am peace," "I am love," or the traditional Sanscrit *mantra* "OM" are good examples. Once a phrase is chosen, it is best not to change it, for that will just add to the mindtalk or internal dialogue. Burning some incense can also be supportive of the meditation; frankincense is a favorite used in the Christian tradition, Sandlewood is a good traditional Eastern incense.

Whether a simpler or deeper approach is taken to meditation, it is important to relax into the breathing and the affirmation. The mind will naturally ramble for a while. When the mind's wanderings are noticed, rather than criticize ourselves, it is best to simply observe in a detached manner where the mind has been drawn, then return the focus immeditately to the breath and the affirmation.

Early benefits of meditation include general stress management and an excellent balancing of the physical, mental and emotional aspects of our lives. In time, meditation yields a greater understanding of ourselves, a deeper connection to our Higher Self and our Higher Power and, with practice, the ability to merge into a deep and profound peace. It matters not whether we approach meditation as a formal discipline or if we make it an easy and informal part of our daily routine. What *is* important is that it is one of our greatest keys to knowing and understanding ourselves, and *that* is an integral part of developing our self-esteem.

EXERCISES

1.   Practice this exercise whenever you can to help develop your intuition and your own connection

to yourself. Start with any decision you may need to make. It may be a decision as simple as the choice of which exit to take on the freeway, or it may be something more significant, such as whether or not to get married. Imagine that your heart is a computer and that your are holding option number one on a floppy disc in your right hand, and option number two on a floppy disc in your left hand.

Now imagine inserting option one into the computer in your heart. Observe the body's response. If the breath stops or slows and the muscles tense, there is a good possibility that the Higher Self is giving a message that says, "This is not your best option." If the body relaxes and expands, and the breathing becomes relaxed and easy, it may be a way that the body is saying that this option "feels good".

Next try option number two. Notice the body's responses. You may want to try both options several times, continuing to compare your responses. As you practice this, your body will become an excellent reflection of your intuitive abilities.

2.   Establish a regular time and place to meditate. Decide what would be a good agreement for you to make with yourself in relation to how much time to spend meditating. Follow the steps for meditating outlined above in Chapter Seven. Notice the difference in your life after one week; after two weeks; after ten years. You'll be amazed.

8

New Programs for the Mind: The Truth

SETTLING INTO SELF-ESTEEM

"The time has come to make the changes I have always wanted to make. No more guilt-tripping myself instead of handling the issues. No more beating myself up rather than taking the steps to get to my goal. No more excuses. No more blaming the other person. No more poor, poor pitiful me. It's time to bite the bullet, gird up my loins, pull myself up by my bootstraps--and go for it."

This is the turning point, that time we all reach sooner or later (in one lifetime or another, some might say) when we've had it with our self-destructive habits and are finally ready to take responsibility for ourselves and create the changes of which we have always dreamed. It's as if our pain has reached critical mass, the point where we have just had enough, and we must either change or die. The death of which we are speaking here may be a physical one--the result of substance abuse, overeating, or the stress of workaholic behavior. Or it may be the emotional and spiritual death resulting from losing oneself in codependency, gambling, spending, raging, or turning our brains over to the television set. We have a choice. Sooner or later we finally have to face the fact that all the external manipulations have not accomplished that which can only be changed from within. This is the magical point where we step out into the always exciting and ever challenging path of personal growth.

We have discussed the dynamics of growth from the perspective of understanding how we took on self-deprecating thought and belief patterns in the past. We have covered the effects of habits, and how habitual thoughts have perpetuated habitual code-pendent and addictive behaviors. We have learned the Reprogramming Process, perhaps the most important technique for unveiling the hidden and untrue negative mindtalk that has been responsible for low self-esteem. And we have considered the new attitudes and habits that support the development of self-esteem. But zipping through a "how-to" book is not the same as developing the "how-to" skills. That takes time, practice, dedication and commitment. As one level of mastery is gained, deeper levels can then be incorporated. The last two chapters of this book address refinement of the attitudes and techniques for living with self-esteem.

It's all well and good to gain insight into our problems; it is another matter to *do* something about them. How often do we swear we will never repeat a given mistake again, only to discover we have repeated it a number of times before we even noticed. When we are going about the process of changing a habit that does not serve us, the first thing we must do, as we have already discussed, is to change our mindtalk about that habit. Remember, all that we create in physical form begins in thought form. We actually choose our thoughts (Hay, 1984) and as such, choose our reality.

Once we have become aware of our mindtalk through the Reprogramming Process, through meditation, and by simply becoming more watchful of our mind and our feelings, we have the raw materials for change. The next step is to do it. That is easier said than done. We have discussed the "benefits" of keeping our old habits, and have observed how difficult it sometimes is to replace that familiar mindtalk that "feels" true with self-esteem based thoughts. So it is important to be aware as we go about our growth that we *will* be confronted by our own resistance. It is necessary to understand that *this resistance is part of the process.* It is only natural that it is not easy to take down the barriers that we have so long used to protect ourselves from pain.

Because we know we will experience resistance within ourselves, our first strategy is to treat ourselves with gentleness. When we are gentle with ourselves, we do not increase our own resistance. We have all observed or participated in arguments where both parties dig in deeper and deeper to their own positions, not because they know they are right, but because they simply do not want to give up. Our own minds can battle like this within us sometimes. So when we are gentle with ourselves, we remove that internal experience of opposition that increases our resistance. As we work on our growth, we are always challenged to discover that balance between pushing ourselves toward new horizons, and not pushing so hard that we dig our heels in and refuse to go forward.

Gentleness is also an aspect of genuine self-esteem. When we are unconditionally loving to ourselves, we recognize when we are doing our best. We do not make ourselves wrong for our mistakes, but instead become our own cheering section. We have all no doubt met, on occasion, a person who was unconditionally loving. What happens to our barriers at those times? They melt. They are no longer needed because we do not feel threatened by that person. In the same way, *when we are patient with ourselves, when we treat ourselves the way we would like others to treat us,* we become our own best friend. Thus our resistance to growth is greatly diminished, and our process of change becomes infinitely easier.

AFFIRMING AND AFFIRMATIONS

The traditional approach to breaking habits and addictions is to "gut it out." It is true that one cannot bypass the necessity of asserting our will and going through the discomfort of withdrawal--whether it be from cocaine, sexual addiction, or the seemingly innocent but codependent behavior of "caretaking" our spouse or children. However, we can simplify the process and make it more gentle by first addressing the beliefs in our mind that perpetuate the addiction. This is one reason that hypnosis is often helpful in habit control. It simply puts us in a relaxed state where we are more easily receptive to positive affirmations about our ability to gain mastery in our lives.

It is obvious that we compound the difficulty of giving up our useless habits when our mindtalk works against our intention to free ourselves. We work against ourselves when our minds say, even on a subconsious level, "I just can't kick this habit," "I'll never be able to make decisions by myself," "I can't handle this pain," "Alcohol is stronger than I am," "I enjoy smoking too much to quit," and "I'm too weak." Our mindtalk may take the form of excuses, rationalizations, denial, or low self-esteem coupled with hopelessness. But it does not matter what form it takes; we can change it. If we are to live our lives in a truly creative way, we must take a step beyond recognizing the false beliefs from the past; they must be replaced with that which we wish to create.

Affirmations are statements that acknowledge that powerful aspect of ourselves which is grounded in self-esteem. Affirmations are the *positive, self-esteem based affirming mindtalk which we use to replace the negative, self-effacing and destructive mindtalk of the past.* The use of affirmations was greatly popularized by Sondra Ray in her book *I Deserve Love* (1987). Although she does not label it as such, this is a book in which she addresses much of the mindtalk that is typical of low self-esteem.

When and how are affirmations used? The answer is, "all the time" and "any way." *Perhaps the most important time to make use of an affirmation is the moment we notice our negative mindtalk.* As we become adept at using the Reprogramming Process, we gradually become familiar with our "favorite" self-destructive mindtalk. Soon it is simply a matter of, "Oh, it's *that* one--about how 'no one loves me,' again." As we regularly apply the Reprogramming Process, we get quicker at noticing those almost imperceptible little nasty things we say about ourselves. It is when the big and the little events occur in an average day, that inputting affirmations is most effective. When we nip the negative mindtalk at the bud; we reverse it before it begins to take a toll on our self-esteem. If, each and every time we hear untrue statements in our minds, we immediately replace them with meaningful affirmations (even if those affirmations do not "feel" true), we are doing the most powerful work possible on our self-esteem.

Returning to the concept of overcoming habits

and addictions, it bears emphasizing here that by replacing the negative mindtalk with affirmations, we lay the crucial foundation for any healing. When the mind is "overheard" to say, "I just can't kick this habit," it can be replaced by "I *can* kick this habit. I know I can. I'm a powerful person and I know I can do it." Even though at first it may seem artificial, in time the mind will release the many years of resistance and open up to those truths. For, *they are truths*. Each one of us has the capability for mastery. Thus, we can replace, "I'll never be able to make decisions by myself," with, "I *can* make my own decisions," or, "Sometimes it's scary and lonely but my decisions are just as valid as anyone else's; I choose to honor my choices."

"I can't handle this pain," is one of the most dangerous pieces of mindtalk, for it gives us "permission" to engage in our habits and addictions. A self-esteem affirming statement would be, "I don't like this pain, but I am able and willing to experience it, for I know it has important information for me." The mindtalk, "Alcohol is stronger than I am," can be countered with affirmations such as "I am a strong person; I am gaining power over my addiction; and, I can choose not to give my power to alcohol." "I enjoy smoking too much to quit," can be replaced with, "I enjoy fresh air more than smoke; I am calm and comfortable in social situations; and, my health is more important to me than my addiction." "I'm too weak," might be replaced with "I am strong; I am becoming more and more powerful; it's OK to be weak sometimes--that doesn't mean I'm a weak person."

Another way to use affirmations is to repeat them or write them regularly. As has been mentioned before, they can be repeated while meditating; they can also be thought or said aloud while doing any simple activity, such as driving, exercising, or doing the dishes. Another beneficial and powerful use of affirmations is to "program" the mind with positive thoughts and visualizations immediately before sleep. This way the subconscious mind can go to work on those new beliefs while we are sleeping. This can be done by writing affirmations before retiring in the evening, by saying them as we are falling asleep, or by playing a guided meditation or hypnosis tape containing appropriate positive statements at bedtime. Guided meditation and hypnosis tapes should not be played while driving, for they create too relaxed a state to be safe. However, subliminal hypnosis tapes can be played while cooking, cleaning, gardening, sewing, or doing other jobs around the home.

Keep in mind that it is of no benefit to use false affirmations. We want to live in awareness of the truth of our own abilities and power, not in fantasy. Virginia Satir (1988) refers to self-esteem as the ability to treat oneself with love, dignity *and* reality. Thus we want to make sure that our affirmations are statements which can actually be manifested. If we say, "I can do anything, or everybody loves me, or I never make mistakes," we are only grounding ourselves in additional false mindtalk and again placing unfulfillable demands on ourselves.

Absolutes are not true in the case of negative mindtalk; neither are they accurate in the case of positive mindtalk. We do not want to run our lives according to a false set of limitations, nor do we want to pretend we have none. As we value ourselves more and more, we move into a balance where we stretch and extend our abilities, and at the same time acknowledge our genuine limitations--loving ourselves unconditionally in both situations. This becomes our formula for successful living: *doing that which we love and that at which we are skilled, plus acknowledgement of the limitations over which we have no control, plus self-esteem, equals success.*

THE "IT'S OK" PROCESS

Part of our work in creating self-esteem is allowing and honoring all the different parts of ourselves. Sometimes we can accept certain weaknesses while others remain unacceptable to us. For example, we may be able to gently work on our issue of shyness, but feel very intolerant of our anger. Or we may see the fact that we talk a great deal as an amusing idiosyncrasy, but be greatly ashamed of a limp. As we come to see ourselves as unconditionally lovable, *all* our emotional, mental and physical parts become acceptable to us. We get "OK" with the parts we can't change and those on which we are still working.

A simple variation on the Reprogramming Process and a means for hearing the mindtalk while acknowledging any internal resistance that might come up, is a process I call the "It's OK" Process. It was conceived by my friend Ed McGinnis and inspired by *The Course in Miracles* (1975). It starts in a similar manner to the Reprogramming Process. When experiencing or remembering an event, we first allow the emotions to surface and listen carefully to our mindtalk. This time, for each thought or emotion that arises, we simply say to ourselves that those feelings or mindtalk are OK. In other words, we give ourselves unconditional acceptance. We then listen for the next feeling or mindtalk that surfaces, and again acknowledge that having that feeling or thought is OK. The steps, again, to the It's OK Process are:

1. When an event occurs or is remembered, fully experience the feelings--physical and emotional.

2. Listen to the statements of feelings or
    mindtalk
3. After each statement, say, "It's OK that I feel
    or think..." and repeat the statement or
    feeling.
4. Notice what new mindtalk or feeling arises
    repeating steps 2 and 3 until there is a
    feeling of acceptance and resolution.

For example, Marion was recently divorced and
was facing life as a single mother of two. While she
had worked from time to time, she had never needed
to support herself. As she began looking for a job, she
was not only overwhelmed by the new and challenging lifestyle she was facing, but by all of her fears and
convictions that she couldn't handle it. Her internal
resistance made the future appear to her even more
difficult. She used the It's OK Process to help lighten
that load. It went, in part, as follows:

MINDTALK OR FEELING   IT'S OK

I can't do it by myself.   It's OK that I think I
                               can't do it alone.

I'll fall apart.   It's OK if I fall apart.
I'll turn into a raging   It's OK to have all my
  maniac.   feelings
I won't be a good mother.   It's OK if I'm not the
                                 perfect mother.

I'm afraid.   It's OK to be afraid.
I won't be able to handle   It's OK if I can't handle
  it all .   it all.
I' ll make too many   It's OK to make
  mistakes   mistakes
I'll have to ask for help   It's OK to ask for help

For Marion, giving herself permission to fall apart, make mistakes, and ask for help took off a major portion of the pressure of going out on her own. When she could accept that she would probably not perform all her new functions perfectly, she could then be more comfortable with herself as she took her first hesitant steps into single parenthood.

Just as in the Reprogramming Process when self-esteem based statements do not always "feel" true, so it may also occur in the It's OK Process that some of our thoughts and feelings may not "feel" OK. It may take repeating the process a number of times in relation to different events in order to actually move to a point where we can genuinely accept what is inside of us. It is important to remember that the purpose of the It's OK Process is to acknowledge and accept what is inside of us, not to perpetuate untruths. It is not a substitute for the Reprogramming Process, where the purpose is to expose and eliminate old negative interpretations by which we have lived. The It's OK Process works specifically for areas of our lives that we would like to transform, but have not yet been able to make those changes. It helps us to remove our own internal fight against ourselves, freeing us to work on our own issues in a more loving and constructive manner.

THE FORGIVENESS PROCESS
Whereas the It's OK Process is a way to accept ourselves with our weaknesses, the Forgiveness Process helps us to let go of genuine or supposed errors that we have made. We all "lose it", from time to time--blow up at our kids, say hurtful things to our partner, act revengeful, or hide from resolving problems with friends. If we are already well grounded in our self-esteem, we simply acknowledge our mistake, de-

termine how we can do it differently next time, make amends to those whom we have hurt, then move on with our lives. With self-esteem, self-forgiveness is relatively automatic; we understand that our errors are part of the process of living and growing. However, if we have not yet learned to have unconditional high regard for ourselves, we are painfully aware of our errors and have a hard time releasing them. We feel guilty, and tend to run a stream of mindtalk reinforcing low self-esteem.

The Forgiveness Process is a way of letting go of our errors; it is a way of practicing, step by step, to leave the field of self-recrimination and enter into freedom. No healing is complete without forgiveness. Yet it must be kept in mind that the groundwork for forgiveness is self-esteem. If we are "not good enough," we are automatically, and by definition, unforgivable. Unconditional self-regard means we are automatically forgivable, for errors are a natural part of our humanness as well as our growth. Self-esteem is the foundation for forgiveness. The Forgiveness Process is a way to help awaken that awareness when it is needed. The steps to the Forgiveness Process are:

1. See the error clearly; re-experience it with all the senses; re-experience the emotions connected with it. Notice all the ramifications of that error. Now give the error a symbolic form and place it before you.
2. Imagine reaching out and embracing that error. Remind yourself that errors are a part of the growth process. Imagine filling the error with white light. Hold the error close and fill it with love until it seems that the error has been healed.
3. In your mind or aloud, ask yourself and all

those involved for forgiveness.
4. Next, forgive the error, including the thoughts and actions involved. Remind yourself that you were doing the best you could at the time. Forgive yourself and forgive anyone else involved.
5. Receive forgiveness. Let it in. Feel the mind and body filling with peace, understanding and acceptance.
6. Commit to yourself not to repeat this error again. Visualize your life as it would be without that error. And, if the error is repeated, also repeat the Forgiveness Process.
7. Acknowledge yourself for work well done.

THE MIRROR PROCESS

The most important person in the world for us to love and respect, is ourself. Yet often, when we look in the mirror, we are not even aware of that person before us. Or if we are, we look only at the imperfections. Our eyes dart from mole to scar to crooked eyelid to enlarged pore. We get disgusted, run some mindtalk, do the best we can to fix what we see as flaws, sigh, and take off for our day's chores. The person behind the face receives no notice.

Making a connection with that person in the mirror can be a powerful way to develop a loving relationship with ourselves. Louise Hay (1984) healed herself of cancer, and has taught thousands of others the techniques by which she achieved that healing. To her, mirror work is one of the most important methods to learn about loving and healing ourselves.

Take five minutes and look deeply into those eyes in the mirror. Notice how very much we can read in the eyes. All of the hurts and joys, even the thoughts, are reflected in those "windows of the soul". Notice what feelings are reflected there. Are those eyes soft and receptive, or does it feel like staring at a stone wall? Get to know that person on a deeper level.

Now, speak aloud to that person in the mirror, saying, "I love you. I respect you. You are wonderful and worthwhile. You are lovable. You deserve good things. I love you exactly the way you are." Notice the reaction. Does the person in the mirror receive and let in that acknowledgement, or does it get shut out? If there is resistance, be persistent. For some people this is not an easy exercise. If we have spent many years not loving ourselves and filling ourselves with shame, we may be afraid to look into our own eyes, for there is only condemnation reflected there. But, we can change that by our will and by our choice. We can decide *now* to love ourselves no matter what.

When I first learned of the mirror process, I challenged myself to do this process for five minutes a day for two months. For the first two weeks my mind countered every positive statement with a negative one. "I love you." ("No I don't.") "You are wonderful." ("What a creep!") "I love you just the way you are." ("What a joke!")

Then one day I noticed how hard and steely cold those eyes were. I was sick of looking in the mirror. It was depressing. "Boy, I sure am hard on myself," I thought. Then it hit me: I didn't have to treat myself so badly! I could treat myself nicely. That poor person in the mirror was starved for affection, and *I* was holding out. All I had to do was give that hungry being before me some love! So this time, when I said "I love you; I think you are wonderful," I really meant it. Amazingly enough, the transformtion in those eyes in the mirror was instantaneous--they glistened with love and joy. Ever since then I have never had to be sad or depressed for long, for I always know that when I need love, I can always look in the mirror and make sure I get it.

BRINGING THE DREAM INTO REALITY

As we change what we think, we change our reality. We change it by changing what we create and by changing how we perceive what we have created. Before we learn to take responsibility for ourselves, we believe that our problems are caused by other people. If they just did things the *right* way (the way *we* think it should be) then we'd be happy. But as we learn to take responsibility for our thoughts and feelings, we soon learn that we create our lives by a kind of self-fulfilling prophesy. We think life will be a certain way, we act accordingly, and naturally, others treat us as if what *we* believe were true. Our body language, our tone of voice, our choice of words, and even the subtle psychic projections of our thoughts let everyone know how we see the world. People who think the world is a miserable place draw everyone into their "dark cloud." People who know the world is full of love are surrounded by loving people.

If we understand this principle, we can make use of it. Sales seminars are in great abundance these days because this basic concept can be applied to help sell a product. A better application of this philosophy, however, is to use it to improve our lives. Ceasing the negative mindtalk and replacing it with positive affirmations is one step. But we can take it further. The more we identify what we want and visualize it coming about, the more we are actively participating in creating our reality instead of experiencing life as a victim. Either way, *we are the creators; we either create life unconsciously out of the morass of unexamined mental habits, or, we create it consciously by the application of our will and choice.*

In order to consciously create, we must first be clear on what we *want* to create. Fred wanted a job. He actually already had one, working for a printing company, but they only used his services for about ten to fifteen hours a week, so he couldn't count on a specific income. Over a two month period he interviewed for a number of diverse positions. He turned down offers as an art director, a camera man, a typesetter and a paste-up artist. Finally he asked for my help. In truth, all he needed was to identify exactly what he wanted, for he obviously had no trouble being offered jobs. What he realized was that he liked his current position because it was only a few blocks from his home and he enjoyed the diversity of his art and printing responsibilities. His main concern was that he was not working enough hours. As we discussed it, he realized that he wanted to stay in his current position and work a specified number of hours. He appoached his boss, who immediately agreed to the increased time. Fred had found the job he was looking for by simply becoming clear within himself as to what would work best for him.

When we are confused about what we want, we create confusion. It is said that if we don't know where we are going, that is where we'll end up. Conversely, if we are very clear on our goal and constantly hold the image of its creation in our minds, we will sooner or later bring it about. We usually do not understand the incredible potential we hold in our own minds. By consciously and actively projecting thoughts for our own well-being, health, and happiness, we can actually make them happen.

We have already discussed ways of changing our patterns by using affirmations and guided meditations before or as we are retiring in the evening. We can do the same thing with visualizations. One very dynamic way to do this is called "Treasure Mapping". Cut out magazine pictures, preferably color, that represent desired goals or creations. Paste them on a page. Write some related affirmations next to them. Use a different page for each goal. Take a few minutes before going to sleep each night to look at those images. That's all! Do it for a month or two. The subconscious mind gradually gets used to the idea that we deserve our highest good. Negative beliefs about those goals gradually drop away, and ways to create those goals become apparent. The year that I attended graduate school full time, I did not know how I would possibly get by financially. But I created a treasure map for unexpected income and, while I was at it, a vacation in a beautiful place. I received a very generous scholarship, and was also asked to accompany a friend, all expenses paid, on a tour of the Ozark Mountains. It was wonderful.

"Programming' our minds in this way is particularly effective as we are falling asleep, because it makes use of the receptive alpha brain waves which are characteristic of a relaxed state. But there is no reason to limit ourselves to that time. We can visualize that which we wish to create at any time of the day. I had decided I wanted a Honda Accord. Someone suggested I put a photo of an Accord on the dashboard of the car I was driving at the time to help me visualize it. The only photo I could find that day was one of a Mazda 626, but I figured that was close enough. I kept the picture there for about a month before it fell off and got buried under the seat. Some time later when I did get a new car, and as I was cleaning out the old one to sell it, I found that picture. I hadn't even thought about it when I had purchased the new car, but, you guessed it--I had bought a Mazda.

WE CREATE OUR LIVES! If we know and understand these principles, we can use them to create love and joy and peace, not only in our own little corners of the world, but on the planet as a whole. We DO have the power. We can choose that at each and every moment. We can choose it now...and now...and now.

EXERCISES

1.   Are you still using the Reprogramming Process? Choose one event from the last day or so and repeat the Reprogramming Process. After you have identified and reprogrammed the mindtalk identify two or three affirmations which would be appropriate to counter these negative statements about the self. Repeat those affirmations for five minutes each evening for one week.

2.   Use the same event and follow the steps above for the It's OK Process. Now try the It's OK Process with a different event. What do you notice?

3.   Return to Exercises 1 and 2 in Chapter Five. Using what you now know, on the right hand side write affirmations to reprogram the criticisms, and statements of acceptance and choice to replace the demands.

4.   Think of an area of your life or an aspect of your personality which you still do not accept. What errors do you keep repeating in relation to that issue? Follow the steps to the Forgiveness Process and observe what you experience.

5.   Write a short story about your future as you have always dreamed it to be. Allow yourself to fully describe and visualize exactly what you would like. Do not hold back any fantasy because it seems too far-fetched. Make sure you include specific experiences about your physical, emotional, mental, and spiritual well-being.

6.   Create a treasure map. Put it on your refrigerator, bedroom wall, or closet door--some place where you will look at it often! Look at it immediately before going to sleep each night for one or two months. Notice the results.

9

Self-Esteem and Healthy Relationships

BETTER RELATIONSHIPS START WITH ME

When we heal ourselves, we heal our personal relationships, our families, and our planet. The healing element, whether the affliction be mental, emotional, or physical, is ultimately love. As we give ourselves that unconditional acceptance and high regard that is the basis of self-esteem, we change how we perceive our world. Thus, when we love ourselves, we experience ourselves as surrounded by love. This changes how we act, how we speak, our tone of voice, our posture, the expressions on our face, and what we expect from other people.

When we are grounded in our own self-esteem, the dynamics of our interaction with others also change. We move from codependency to healthy relationships with other people, our jobs, our bodies, our world--and ourselves. Since we take responsibility for ourselves, we no longer need to demand that another person treat us a certain way. Since we can acknowledge our own mistakes, we are more tolerant of others' errors. With the burden of self-incrimination and low self-regard lifted from our own shoulders, we remove it as well from where we have also inappropriately placed it--on the shoulders of those around us. Because we take responsibility for ourselves, we can live a life free of blame and guilt directed at ourselves and at other people. In doing so, we find ourselves no longer in opposition to others. We become safe and easy to be around.

If we are to heal our lives, it is necessary to understand on the deepest levels that *the only person we are responsible for changing or even can change, is ourselves*. Even children make their own choices regarding thoughts and behavior. At best, a parent wields great influence and provides the environment for growth. How often do we wish that our partner, our kids, our in-laws, our boss, and even our friends were different? How often do we have those thoughts without ever really considering that it is our own perspective that is in need of change? We like to think, when we are uncomfortable, that we can influence those around us to behave in a different manner so that we will feel better. This thinking is ineffective not only because of the resulting opposition, resistance and power plays that it creates, but because it does not address the primary problem: If I am uncomfortable, then I'm the one who needs to change.

This premise cannot be emphasized enough. And often, it is a hard pill to swallow. At times, the other person's behavior seems clearly unkind, immoral, or downright abusive. It takes a constant turning within to remind ourselves that we are the creators of our reality, and to *ask ourselves by what habit and belief did we draw this experience to us.*

The people around us are mirrors of our internal experience. If we believe we are ugly and unattractive, we will choose lovers who are constantly looking at other, more attractive bodies, or spouses who complain about our appearance. If we think we are inept, we will find jobs where our boss gets impatient with our every move. If we think we are responsible for other people's feelings, we will find ourselves being blamed at every turn. Thus, if we don't like what is coming to us externally, it is time to check and see if we are not feeding ourselves with the same thing internally.

Why on earth would we set ourselves up like that, we might ask? It does seem a bit masochistic at first glance. But our Higher Self, that part of us operating for our greatest growth, has a wonderful ability to draw the lessons to us which we need. Sometimes those lessons come in an easy and loving way. But, unfortunately, we can be rather thick-skulled at times. If we don't learn the lessons the easy way, the messages are brought to us in louder and louder--thus more and more painful--ways.

So often we find ourselves crying out, "WHY does this keep happening to me?" It keeps happening because we did not see the need for growth when the messages were quiet and easy. It is as if our Higher Self had the ability, unlike the light on the dashboard of our car, to turn up the intensity so that we can better see that beacon for change and growth. The continued and increased pain is like buzzers, bells and flashing lights going off on the dash. NOW will we notice, or will we continue on with our eyes blind to the signals that call for growth and change?

The people in our lives reflect who and what we are. We have drawn them to us to help us see and hear better what we think. When we experience ourselves to be in love, we are actually loving ourselves unconditionally. That is then reflected in the people within our environment, and we interpret those feelings as love coming from others. Similarly, when we live in anger, we find other angry people and bring them into our sphere of influence. While we do not realize it, we subconciously do this so we will face and ultimately heal our own anger. When we don't like what we see in another, most often the irritant is actually that we are observing that person act out an issue we have not yet handled in ourselves. We are like a closed system, often unable to perceive ourselves clearly. *Therefore, in order to better create evolution for ourselves, we externalize our issues by finding others who reflect them* (Del Prince, 1989). This helps us to better see and ultimately heal that which lies within.

Kay would feel exasperated that her husband Don would rattle on and on, and never listen to her. As he spoke, she would hum, sigh, and daydream to get back at him for not listening to her. What she did not notice was that she was not listening to him either. Randy had a large number of consecutive sexual relationships. He complained that women were never caring and that they never did anything to make his involvement with them worth his while. He had forgotten to notice that his own caring and input was almost nil. What we receive is usually a mirror, though often in a different form, of what we give.

I once was a part of a group of about twenty people who decided that its members would take turns being in "the hot seat", so that everyone could air their gripes about each other. The ground rules were to be truthful, but not hurtful. By the time we had gotten around to about the seventh person, we discovered a pattern. Each person who was about to speak would pause for quite a while, then preface his or her statement with, "Well, I actually do this too, but what really irritates me about you is...." They would then proceed to describe a behavior or habit that we all knew to be one of that person's greatest shortcomings.

We all had to laugh, for what we had discovered was that what bothered us most about other people was what bothered us most about ourselves. If we notice our irritations and hurts about others' behaviors, our greatest path to clarity is to ask ourselves how we do that very same thing.

When we take responsibility for our lives, as much as we may wish the other person would be kinder or more loving, our first work is always to check and see if we are being the loving person we want that other person to be for us. Are we being the nourishing mother, the supportive father, the romancing lover that we want the other to be? Are we expecting other people to be something we ourselves do not take responsibility to be?

When we have created the love within, it will, by natural law, be created outside of us as well. In the *Bible* it is written that we reap what we sow. In Eastern terms it is called the law of Karma. It is a universal truth that "what goes 'round, comes 'round." To heal what comes in, we must look to what we put out.

A few questions always come up about this principle in regards to people who appear to be genuine victims of circumstance or abuse. Yet, I do not believe there are exceptions to this law. I would answer as follows. First, we must keep looking deeper within us to find those pockets of unkindness and abuse that may still linger within us, even though they may be carefully disguised as caretaking, helping, pleasing, righteousness, diplomacy, or solving others' problems. Second, we must look to our thoughts, keeping in mind that thoughts are the primary creative force. We may not *do* hate, but if we *think* hate, we will reap the same results. Finally, where no obvious karmic reason can be found, such as in the case of abuse of small children, or starvation, or natural catastrophes, the only reasonable explanation for me is the concept that the karma, or reaping what we sow, carries over from previous lifetimes.

While I have studied reincarnation from both the Eastern religious and Western research perspectives, it was an Episcopal priest who first pointed out to me that this concept once had a place in early Christianity (Flew, 1979). I have debated whether to discuss in a primarily psychological book, the idea that the "good and bad luck" we experience now are actually the results of our own kind and unkind actions in past lives. Such a discussion raises issues of religion and personal belief systems. Yet, I know a number of psychotherapists who privately believe that a study of past lives does offer important information for emotional healing. Few, however, are willing to risk publicly acknowledging this perspective. I believe that if we counseling professionals are to ask our clients to learn to be vulnerable and truthful with themselves and others, then we must do the same. Interestingly enough, as I was writing the above paragraphs, *two* therapists called and asked me to facilitate past life regressions for them.

However, it is not my intention here to suggest that the readers take on the belief in reincarnation. This is a personal matter which does not affect any of the other concepts contained within these pages. I will say, however, that where traditional psychotherapy seems to be unable to address or explain what appears to be unwarranted abuse, a look into past lives will often uncover explanations that cannot be found in our current life. In my own case, my father often directed a great deal of anger towards me as a child; to me it did not make sense. When I was regressed to a lifetime where I was abusive to him, I experienced a deep sense of guilt and remorse. As I forgave myself, I also forgave him. I began to treat him with a kindness I did not give him in that earlier lifetime. I started to see him as the patient and gentle person he was at *that* time. And, as indicated earlier, our relationship has become one of great love and caring.

Yet the time frame with which we are working is not the most important element, for the principles are the same. What we give out comes back to us. When we do not like what we are receiving, it is time to look within to see what we are giving. It is not a matter of blaming ourselves but of taking responsibility for our own growth. *When we take responsibility for ourselves, we step out of the victim role.* Thus, if we want to improve our relationships, the first thing to work on is ourselves. When we are clear, loving, and well centered in our own self-esteem, we make wise choices regarding who we spend our time with, *and*, we relate to others in a loving and supportive manner.

RELATIONSHIPS AS OPPORTUNITIES TO GROW

As we have seen above, we actually create our relationships so that the other person becomes the mirror through which we see ourselves. When we are loving, this helps to create a cyclical feedback system that is mutually supportive to both individuals. The most obvious example of this is when people first "fall in love." Each one becomes aware of the positive aspects of the self as reflected through the mirror of the other; mindtalk about not being enough is temporarily put aside.

On the other hand, when there are doubts, negativity and criticism toward the self, our lack of alignment with ourselves assures a lack of alignment with those around us. This sets up a natural state of opposition, where, if we are fighting and rejecting that which is within us, then the person before us, as the mirror of ourselves, becomes the focus of that struggle.

It thus becomes obvious that getting the other person to change does not address the real problem. One of the saddest lessons we have gained from the results of our current high divorce rate, is that people divorce one spouse only to find themselves in relationship with another person with whom the dysfunctional dynamics are essentially, or exactly, the same. *When we do not change ourselves, we may change mirrors, but the reflection remains the same.*

So what are we to do when the inevitable disagreements, arguments, hurts and anger between friends and loved ones arise? The codependent answer is to caretake, dominate, manipulate and/or avoid--act cheerful when we feel hurt, stuff our feelings, avoid confrontation, bully the other to get what we want, withhold love, lie, or otherwise attempt to control the other. But as we have seen, these behaviors bring quick fixes--bandaids with no substantial healing, cover-up rather than growth and resolution.

Relationships are one of the primary means available for learning. Will we run from our greater potential by hiding in the illusion of codependency, or will we embrace the work that leads us to the happiness we all crave? We can give up on our mate (and ourselves), or we can use the hard times as fertilizer for growth. In our relationships, we humans are like two pieces of rough sandpaper that are rubbed together; we are gradually smoothed by the lessons learned in our interactions with each other.

We tend to think of the difficult spots in our relationships as negative. We look to see who is right and who is wrong, and for the most part attempt to position ourselves so that we can be seen as right, (unless for manipulative purposes it serves us better to be seen as wrong.) But in truth, it is the difficult times that, like the light on the dashboard of our car, lead us to the resolutions that ultimately bring the improvements we would like. I have worked with so many couples who come into therapy with the perspective that, "If we can't work this out, its all over." Yet to me, the fact that they have chosen to get assistance means that they care enough for each other to do what it takes to work out their problems. And that is what they usually do.

The real question always is, "Do I want to be right, or do I want to resolve our differences?" Sometimes we become so enmeshed in our disagreements, we lose track of the fact that love and resolution of the problems are what we really want. Our egos, which function to help maintain our individuality, can also tie us painfully to our separateness and estrangement. In the heat of controversy, we become afraid, our minds fill with negative mindtalk both about ourselves and others, and we lose track of what is really important to us.

Yet, I have never met anyone who did not want to be a loving and caring person. When we interpret difficult events in the context that we care about each other, it is not that difficult to say, "I'm sorry, what I did was not kind," or, "Excuse me for interrupting; please continue," or, "We don't seem to see eye to eye on this, but I do want to know your feelings about it."

In creating good relationships with others, it is necessary to remember the greater goal. When we become shortsighted, we forget that our own growth is more important than being right. We forget that creating a loving, healthy and supportive relationship is more rewarding than our comfortable old codependent patterns. I once knew a very wise old Indian swami who had two important mottos which he abbreviated KIV and DIN--"Keep (the goal) in view" and "Do it now." We often think it is fine to get around to creating quality in our lives tomorrow. Yet each and every day is a new opportunity to create the quality we want now. We do not know when our last moment on this earth will come. We must seize the opportunity at each moment. Every obstacle is the gift of a new opportunity to live in joy, in peace, in love. Go for the quality. And do it now.

THE COMMUNICATION PROCESS

We have talked about two very private and personal ways to create healthy relationships. The first is to look always to our own lessons instead of looking to change the other. The second is to recognize and make use of existing differences of opinions, knowing that they are, in fact, stepping stones to our own growth. This, of course, does not mean that we cease any attempts at working together to create a more dynamic and satisfying relationship. Nor does it mean we should stuff our feelings or abandon our needs and desires.

Quite the opposite: Expressing what is true for us is absolutely essential in order to create a healthy relationship. In *Why Am I Afraid To Tell You Who I Am?*, John Powell (1969), suggests that it is common for us to believe that others cannot tolerate emotional honesty in our communications. We thus give ourselves permission not to be clear or honest about our real feelings and thoughts, defending this behavior with the rationalization that we are avoiding hurting others or that we are being noble, when in fact we are merely settling for superficial relationships.

Sharing our true feelings and thoughts is a statement of our self-esteem and of our trust in a relationship. It says, "I'm going to allow the real me to communicate with the real you; let's take the barriers down." In Powell's view, telling the truth is the greatest kindness we can offer another person. And, communication of this caliber is most effective when we have done our own homework and are well aware of how our own issues and weaknesses play into interpersonal differences. It is also most effective when we share within the *context* of the perspective that the relationship and the other person are important to us.

Jan and Stuart, two close friends, had decided to meet for lunch. But a miscommunication about when they would get together, coupled with a last minute meeting that ran late, resulted in Jan arriving forty-five minutes later than Stuart. He was angry, and an argument ensued in which he accused her of being thoughtless and she accused him of lacking understanding about a situation that could not be helped. Both clung to their own positions.

Finally Jan noticed that the context of their friendship had been lost. She took a deep breath and put her hand on Stuart's and said, "Stuart, you are very dear to me; I'm very sorry that this miscommunication happened. I could have called when I knew I'd be late. My mindtalk was that because what I had to do was so important, you shouldn't mind waiting. That wasn't an appropriate assumption to make. I'm sorry you ended up waiting so long." Stuart's anger was immediately dissipated; he thanked Jan for bringing them both back to center, and apologized for his anger and mistrust of her. The rest of the lunch was a delight, and both felt closer to each other for the fact that they had aired and cleared the differences between them.

What this interaction demonstates is how to put clarity in a relationship as a priority over having to be perceived as "right." The *first step* for anyone involved in a disagreement is to *notice* if the discussion has moved away from communication to opposition and negative feelings. The *second step* is a true act of both self-esteem and love, for it involves being willing to move out of the perspective of opposition, and into a position of alignment with what is best for both parties and the relationship. Here we take a moment to disengage from the disagreement, and *acknowledge our caring for the other person* and our desire for a good relationship between us. We are putting the difficult interaction into the greater context of a caring connection.

The *third step* involves going back to our corners, as it were, and *becoming clear within ourselves* exactly what our own mindtalk or lack of clarity within the situation might be. This is a very appropriate time to make use of the Reprogramming Process. This may mean taking a quick look to see what is going on inside of us, or we may need to take some time away from the other person in order to better gain clarity.

So often when we are in a disagreement with another person--we may be complaining about the dishes not being done, or defending ourselves against accusations of unequal treatment--but underneath there are usually deeper issues where our mind is saying "That person doesn't love or respect me; I'm not lovable; I don't deserve good treatment; I'm not good enough." If we stay focused on what we don't like about the other person, we ignore what are important and very real issues for ourselves. By being honest with *ourselves* about what is going on inside of us, we not only can heal our own lives, but we can allow genuine communication to occur with another person.

In codependent patterns, we attempt to feel and say what we think others will want from us in order to win their respect and caring or to get what we want from them. Although we generally learned this style of interaction as an adaptation to painful situations when we were young, it is, nonetheless, a manipulative technique which dishonors ourselves and is based on a lack of trust of the other person. In a healthy relationship, we choose to be honest with ourselves, admitting our weaknesses and errors because we love ourselves unconditionaly anyway! It is enormously *freeing* to be able to simply say, "Oh, I made a mistake," or, "I was afraid," or, "I am really angry." knowing that we are forgivable and lovable despite our shortcomings.

In *step four* we put our cards on the table; we *share honestly with the other person*, being willing to both acknowledge our own weaknesses or errors in the situation and at the same time let that person know our genuine responses to their statements and actions. This involves being courageous and at the same time vulnerable. We are putting ourselves on the line, and there is no guarantee that the other person will respond in kind.

In the example above, when Jan stepped out of her opposition into the vulnerable position of acknowledging her caring for Stuart and the fact that she could have called, he *might* have continued to be angry. She had no assurance that he, too, would recognize his errors and apologize for his anger and accusations. Yet she took that risk because the relationship was important to her.

When we are honest, we risk. The question is, are we willing to put our integrity and self-respect before manipulation? It means taking away the protective barriers over our hearts and loving both ourselves and others unconditionally. It means, "I will honor my own feelings and perspectives, and, even if my view isn't in alignment with yours, I will still also honor yours." It means, "I will risk the diappointment that I might not get what I want from you, because I respect us both and accept our differences."

In Christ's final days, he was deserted and a-bused, yet he held to the truth as he saw it, not with self-righeousness, but with simple and open honesty. He maintained his vulnerability, and yet he was not without fear; at one point his mindtalk said, "Father, why have You abandoned me?" He spoke the truth, knowing it would not serve his personal interest, but rather a higher purpose, when he answered Pilate, saying "Thou sayest that I am a king. To this end was I born, and for this cause came I into the world, that I should bear witness unto the truth. Every one that is of the truth heareth my voice." (John, 19:37) This, clearly, was not a statement that would win him popularity at that moment. Yet he kept his heart open. He understood that the others simply could not see things as he did: "Forgive them, for they know not what they do." He was a model for us in maintaining both vulnerability and honesty, even when things don't seem to go our way.

When we take this fourth step in our communications, we speak the truth as we see it. *We tell the truth about what we feel, think, fear, and want* from the situation, recognizing that the other person may feel, think, and want something different. In order to stay in this place of openness and vulnerability, it helps us to be gentle with ourselves, to maintain an awareness of the heart area of our body, and to breathe deeply through the difficult parts of the communication. Yet if we do not take courage and speak our truth, we both end up hiding behind protective walls, never knowing what is truly going on with the other and never clearing up the misunderstandings created by the mindtalk we both have.

In speaking our truth--our honest thoughts and feelings--it is best to use "I statements." When we are deep in our mindtalk, we tend to fall into speaking out that mindtalk as if it were truth, and to others it often sounds like accusations: "You don't love me; You never do your share; You hurt me." If we have taken the time to examine our negative mindtalk, we can either simply change it to the truth or we can share it with the other person as *mindtalk*, being clear that what we are saying is our *perception* and not necessarily fact. A simple formula for using "I statements" is to say, "When ---- happened, I felt ----, and my mind said ----. What I want is ----." In this manner, we take full responsibility for our own perceptions, reactions, and desires.

When we use "I statements", what sounds like accusations in the above paragraph, could be more appropriately said as follows: Rather than "You don't love me," we might say, "When you spend the evening watching TV, I feel lonely. I start telling myself that you don't love me. I would like very much if we could set aside some time each night to spend together. How do you feel about that idea?"

Instead of the accusation, "You never do your share," we can say, "I'm feeling overburdened by the workload. Sometimes my mind says I'm just a maid to you. I know that's not true, but I'm not happy with the situation as it is. I would like for us to sit down and talk about it, and make some agreements that would work for both of us. What are your thoughts about this?" "You hurt me" might be put, "I feel very hurt. We need to talk about this more, but right now I

would like it if we could just take time out and give
each other a hug for a few minutes."

As has been mentioned, *other people may or may
not respond the way we want them to, but in claiming our
self-esteem, we are first and foremost concerned with the
caring and respect we have for ourselves*. Then, when we
behave with integrity and love for ourselves and the
other person, we have done as much as we can. If the
other does not respond in the manner we would like,
our best option is to return to an introspective ap-
proach--without blaming ourselves or the other.
Ultimately, in continuing to work with our *own* self-
esteem issues, all things come to balance.

Chances are very good, however, that the other
person will sense our respect and desire for good
communication, and respond with more openness.
The ideal situation, of course, is if both people in a relationship follow these basic communication steps.
But whether this occurs or not is really not at issue;
our real work is creating SELF-esteem, and *we are never really tested in our self-esteem until we continue to hon-
or ourselves even when others in our lives do not*.

The *fifth step* in the communication process is al-
luded to in the reconstruction of the mindtalk sentences above with the questions "How do you feel
about that idea?" and "What are your thoughts about
that?" It is not only necessary that we state our feelings, thoughts, and desires clearly, we also need to *listen carefully to the feelings, thoughts, and desires of the
other person*. If we have first become clear about our
own mindtalk and issues, this will be much easier.

When we are upset, we often want to blurt out
all our feelings and mindtalk; we are not always very
interested in what the other person has to say.
However, if we keep an awareness of the context of
caring in the relationship, we can understand that if

we wish to be heard, we must also be willing to hear. Not only to hear, but to listen deeply, with interest and curiosity, to what is going on inside the other. The most effective listening is being aware not only of the surface words and feelings, which are often distorted when we are upset, but of the deeper feelings, needs and desires of another person.

Part of step five includes, in addition to listening, *letting the other person know we are hearing.* This might mean that if we don't quite understand something (especially if we are having an emotional reaction to it), that we ask for clarification. We might ask the other person to restate what he or she is saying in different words, or we might rephrase it ourselves in a simple manner, and ask if we have understood correctly. In other words, we take responsibility to listen in a deep and heartfelt manner to the other person so that we can understand from *that person's* perspective, not from our own interpretation of his or her perspective. As a psychotherapist, I constantly find that disagreements between individuals are usually a matter of a difference of interpretation that can easily be cleared when both parties genuinely listen to each other.

Step six of the Communication Process is to *repeat steps one through five as necessary, taking turns speaking and listening.* If things get too difficult to be constructive, it is a good idea to go back to steps one, two and three, in order to re-establish the context of caring and to stay introspective about our own issues in the situation.

Here are some other little hints for communication. It is always wise to approach others about delicate issues when they are not occupied physically or emotionally with something else. If the other person is not available to talk, *find and agree upon a specific time* when the issue can be discussed. Sometimes persistence is necessary, especially if the subject is in some way frightening to the other person. It is a good idea to remind each other of the context that, even though the discussion might be difficult, it is important to the relationship.

Avoiding the risk and vulnerability of uncomfortable conversations can result in a "safe" but lonely separateness. A very typical example is that couples often avoid discussing their sexual problems for years, sometimes forever, because it is scary. But we do not have to live with that kind of separation. Sharon Wegscheider-Cruse (1987) believes that couples benefit from taking time on a daily basis to listen to each other and share their feelings. In addition, she suggests that the "no talk" rule be broken so that problems are always discussed and cleared. Learning to fight constructively and fairly also keeps the lines of communication open. Sticking with an issue until it is resolved makes it possible to move on with our lives. Finally, she recommends finding lots of ways to have fun.

Whether we observe the steps to the Communication Process alone or if we agree to share it with another person, we are honoring ourselves and the other by its use. And in doing so, we claim our self-esteem. In review, the steps to the Communication Process are:

1. Notice when a discussion or issue has moved away from clear communication to negative feelings and opposition.
2. Create a positive context for communication by making the choice to acknowledge our caring, love, and respect to the other person and by emphasizing that the relationship is important.
3. Take time out for introspection and repro-

gramming of our own issues and mindtalk.

4. Share honestly our own feelings, errors, fears, thoughts, and desires. Be willing to risk and to be vulnerable while, at the same time, staying in touch with our own self-worth.

5. Listen carefully and understand the other person. Get clarification about parts that are not fully understood. Let the other person know that he or she has been heard by our *hearts* as well as our minds.

6. Repeat steps one through five as needed. Repeat them throughout your life.

TRUE INTIMACY

True intimacy can happen when we create relationships, not from our neediness, but from experiencing ourselves as whole and as valuable. When we have claimed our self-esteem, we honor ourselves and we honor others *unconditionally*. We take the bad with the good. We also know--with humility, not with guilt--that we give the bad with the good. We understand that we are in a dance of humanness, in which we learn and grow together. Intimacy happens when we have enough self-esteem to be open and vulnerable, while yet owning our own truth and power. That way I can be me, you can be you, and we can grow both together and separately (Woititz, 1985). There are no illusions between us. We can rest in the knowledge that we care about ourselves, care about each other, and support our mutual growth.

A good friend of mine, Ron Kaye, wrote to me of a dream he had. This was his dream:

"I am standing in a beautiful meadow with the woman I love. I am wearing formal attire, tux, tails and top hat, and we both hold an earthen bowl in our hands.

"I speak to her, saying, 'We each hold a bowl of brackish water, a perfect lotus floating upon the surface. This is the water of my life. It carries the tears of all my heartaches, the bitterness of all my angers, and the sour tang of all my fears.

"This is the perfect blossom of my spirit, adrift upon, yet untainted by the foul waters.

"Both I offer up to you. Willingly do I drink from your bowl. Joyously do I offer the lotus, as well as the bowl. We share, and we are One."

This image beautifully illustrates the essence of the kind of relationships that are possible when we have claimed our self-esteem. Having self-esteem does not mean being perfect or producing or doing or being anything. It means loving ourselves unconditionally. When we can do that for ourselves, we can do it with the other important people in our lives. True intimacy means we share our strengths and our weaknesses while giving and receiving support for our personal growth with another person.

As we claim our self-esteem we claim our birthright. We begin to create our lives by the power of the positive and loving thoughts we have about ourselves. As we become firm in our knowledge of our self-worth and the power to make beneficial choices for ourselves, we start to create life the way we want it to be. We *can* create for ourselves love, happiness, prosperity, health and joy. Affirm it now: YES, I CAN!

EXERCISES

1. Go back and flip through the pages of this book and copy down each process and exercise.

Doing this will help to set them into your mind so that you can more easily draw on them when you need to.

2.   Use your copy of the processes and exercises in this book as a workbook for yourself. Start at the beginning and do several exercises a day. Each and every time you repeat a process or exercise, you will learn more about yourself and become more accustomed to thinking yourself into self-esteem.

***

References

Adler, A. (1927). *The Practice and Theory of Individual Psychology.* New York: Harcourt Publishing Company.

Alexander, Thea. (1971). *2150 A.D.* Tempe, AZ: Macro Books.

Ball, C. M. (1986). *Self Esteem and Human Development.* Unpublished manuscript, University of Houston Clear Lake, Houston.

Beattie, M. (1987). *Codependent No More.* New York: Harper & Row/Hagelden.

Beck, A. T., Rush, A. J., Shaw, B. F., & Emery, G. (1979). *Cognitive Therapy of Depression.* New York· The Guilford Press.

Burns, D. (1980). *The New Mood Therapy.* New York: NAL Penquin Inc.

Bradshaw, J. (1988). *The Family.* Deerfield Beach, FL: Health Communications, Inc.

Branden, N. (1983). *Honoring the Self.* New York: Bantam Books.

Branden, N. (1961). *The Psychology of Self-Esteem.* Toronto: Bantam Books.

Brown, K. B. & Whitten, R. (1983, August). The Life Training, seminar, Kairos Foundation, Houston.

Brown, K. B. & Whitten, R. (Speakers) (1987). The SEE Course. (Cassette Recordings). San Jose, CA: Kairos Foundation.

Combs, A., & Snygg, D. (1959). *Individual Behavior: A Perceptual Approach to Behavior*. New York: Harper and Bros.

Coopersmith, S. (1981). *The Antecedents of Self-Esteem*. Palo Alto, CA: Consulting Psychologists Press, Inc.

Corey, G. (1986). *Theory and Practice of Counseling and Psychotherapy*. Monterey, CA: Brooks/Cole Publishing Company.

Cormier, W., & Cormier, S. (1985). *Interviewing Strategies for Helpers*. Monterrey, CA: Brooks/Cole Publishing Company.

Coudert, J. (1965). *Advice From A Failure*. Chelsea, MI: Scarlborough House Publishers.

Del Prince, P. (1989, February). Hakomi Skills Group Training. Houston.

Ellis, A. E., & Harper, R. A. (1975). *A New Guide To Rational Living*. North Hollywood, CA: Wilshire Book Company.

Ellis, A. E. (1973). *Humanistic Psychotherapy: The Rational Emotive Approach*. New York: Julian Press.

Ellis, A. E. (1977). "Psychotherapy and the Value of a Being." In A. E. Ellis & R. Grieger (Eds.), *Handbook of Rational Emotive Therapy*. New York: Springer Publishing Company.

Ellis, A. E. (1962). *Reason and Emotion in Psychotherapy*. Secaucus, NJ: Citadel Press.

Flew, A. (1979). *A Dictionary of Philosophy*. New York: St. Martins Press.

Foundation for Inner Peace (1975). *A Course In Miracles:* Vol. 2. Farmingdale, NY: Coleman Graphics.

Friends of Recovery. (1987). *The 12 Steps--A Way Out*. San Diego: Recovery Publications.

Gawain, Shakti. (1978). *Creative Visualization*. New York: Bantam Books Inc.

Glasser, W. (1965). *Reality Therapy*. New York: Harper & Row, Publishers.

Glasser, W. (1969). *Schools Without Failure*. New York:
    Harper & Row, Publishers.
Hay, L. L. (1984). *You Can Heal Your Life*. Santa
    Monica, CA: Hay House.
Helmstetter, S. (1986). *What To Say When You Talk
    To Yourself*. New York: Pocket Books.
Jackson, M. R. (1984). *Self-Esteem and Meaning*.
    Albany, NY: State University of New York Press.
Jampolsky, G. G. (1979). *Love is Letting Go of Fear*
    Berkeley, CA: Celestial Arts.
Lembo, J. M. (1976). *The Counseling Process: A
    Cognitive-Behavioral Approach*. Roslyn Heights, NY:
    Libra Publishing.
Lerner, H. G. (1985). *The Dance of Anger*. New York:
    Harper & Row, Publishers, Inc.
Maslow, A. H. (1962). *Toward a Psychology of Being*.
    Princeton, NJ: D. Van Nostrand Company, Inc.
Maslow, A. H. (1970). *Motivation and Personality*.
    New York: Harper & Row, Publishers.
McCarthy, J., & Goodrich, E. (1980). "The Self-
    Concept from a Phenomenological Perspective." In
    T. D. Yawkey (Ed.), *The Self-Concept of the Young
    Child* (pp. 25-31). Provo, UT: Brigham Young
    University Press.
McDonald, K. A. (1980). "Enhancing a Child's Positive
    Self-Concept." In T. D. Yawkey (Ed.), *The Self-
    Concept of the Young Child* (pp.51-62). Provo, UT:
    University Press.
Napier, A., & Whitaker, C. (1978). *The Family
    Crucible*. New York: Bantam Books.
Phillips, D. A., & Zigler, E. (1980). "Self-Concept
    Theory and Practical Implications." In T. D.
    Yawkey (Ed.), *The Self-Concept of the Young Child*
    (pp. 111-122). Provo, UT: Brigham Young
    University Press.
Powell, J. (1969). *Why Am I Afraid To Tell You Who I
    Am?* Allen, TX: Tabor Publishing.

Ray, S. (1980). *Loving Relationships*. Berkeley, CA: Celestial Arts.

Ray, S. (1987). *I Deserve Love*. Berkeley, CA: Celestial Arts.

Rogers, C. R. (1951). *Client-Centered Therapy: Its Current Practice, Implications, and Theory*. Boston: Houghton Mifflin Company.

Rogers, C. R. (1961). *On Becoming a Person*. Boston: Houghton Mifflin Company.

Rosenberg, M. (1979). *Conceiving the Self*. New York: Basic Books, Inc.

Sanford, L. T., & Donovan, M. E. (1984). *Women and Self-Esteem*. New York: Penquin Book.

Satir, V., & Baldwin, M. (1983). *Satir Step By Step*. Palo Alto, CA: Science and Behavior Books.

Satir, V. (1988). *The New Peoplemaking*. Mountain View, CA: Science & Behavior Books, Inc.

Schaef, Anne W. (1986). *Co-dependence: Misunderstood -- Mistreated*. San Francisco, CA: Harper & Row, Publishers.

Stringer, L. A. (1971). *The Sense of Self*. Philadelphia: Temple University Press.

Wegscheider-Cruse, S. (1987). *Learning To Love Yourself*. Pompano Beach, FL: Health Communications, Inc.

Whitfield, C. L. (1987). *Healing the Child Within*. Deerfield Beach, FL: Health Communications, Inc.

Woititz, J. G. (1985). *Struggle for...Intimacy*. Pompano Beach, FL: Health Communications, Inc.

Wylie, R. C. (1974). *The Self-Concept* (rev. ed.) (Vol. 1.) Lincoln, NE: University of Nebraska Press.

Carolyn Ball is a psychotherapist, teacher, and author of numerous articles on personal growth. In her frequent lectures, workshops, and appearances in the media, she offers practical tools for moving from codependent and addictive dysfunctional patterns into a creative and satisfying lifestyle. Her broad experience in psychology, education, Eastern mysticism, and the Native American spiritual tradition yields unique insight into human nature and ways we can live richer and happier lives during our walk on Planet Earth.

Carolyn Ball is available for seminars and speaking engagements on Self-Esteem, Stress Management, and Team Building for corporations, hospitals, recovery centers and groups who would like to sponsor her. She is also available for private consultations by telephone. Please check the subjects you are interested in below for more information on course content, schedules, and fees.

___ **The Claiming Your Self-Esteem Workshop**
___ **Self-Esteem and Recovery**
___ **Self-Empowerment**
___ **Team Building**
___ **Women and Self-Esteem**
___ **Telephone consultations**

Name _____

Company_____

Address _____

City/State/Zip_____

Telephone _____

Send to:

Carolyn Ball
c/o Celestial Arts
P.O. Box 7327
Berkeley, CA 94707

A powerful companion to this book is the **CLAIMING YOUR SELF Audio Tape,** a guided relaxation for creating a new and powerful reality through changing our thoughts and healing our feelings. It can be purchased through the author for $12.95, plus $2.50 shipping.

☐ Please send me the **CLAIMING YOUR SELF Audio Tape.** I am enclosing my check or money order in the amount of $12.95 for the tape plus $2.50 for shipping.

Name _____

Address _____

City/State/Zip_____

Telephone _____

Send orders to:

Carolyn Ball/CYS Audio Tape
c/o Celestial Arts
P.O. Box 7327
Berkeley, CA 94707

OTHER BOOKS YOU MAY ENJOY...

Blessings in Diguise
by Carolyn Ball, M.A.

Delightfully intuitive and honest, *Blessings* is a testament to one woman's remarkable courage and vision. Built around the author's training with Mary Thunder and other Native American elders, her story unfolds as a series of adventrues into consciousness.
paper, 256 pages

Choose to be Healthy
by Susan Smith Jones, Ph.D.

The choices we make in life can greatly increase our health and happiness—this book details how to analyze one's choices about food, exercise, work, and play, and then use this information to create a better, healthier life.
paper, 252 pages

Choose to Live Peacefully
by Susan Smith Jones, Ph.D.

By nurturing our inner selves and living in personal peace, we can help to bring about global change. In this book, Susan Smith Jones explores the many components of a peaceful, satisfying life—including exercise, nutrition, solitude, meditation, ritual, and environmental awareness—and shows how they can be linked to world peace.
paper, 320 pages

Recovery from Addiction
by John Finnegan and Daphne Grey

Alternative herbal and nutritional therapies for a wide range of addictions, from cigarettes to sugar, from caffeine to hard drugs. Includes first-person accounts of how these treatments have worked for a variety of specific problems.
paper, 192 pages

Healing the Addictive Mind
by Lee Jampolsky, Ph.D.

The first book to use lessons from *A Course in Miracles* as a tool for overcoming addictive behaviors, including chemical dependency and codependent relationships. Includes daily exercises for overcoming harmful patterns and gaining spiritual peace.
paper, 172 pages

Addiction to Love
by Susan Peabody

A simple, practical, step-by-step guide for those who find themselves in destructive or codependent relationships. The author, herself a recovering love addict, teaches popular and effective seminars on the topic.
paper, 120 pages   A TEN SPEED PRESS BOOK

Self Esteem
by Virginia Satir

A simple and succinct declaration of self worth which serves as inspiration and affirmation for anyone who needs a "quick hit" of positive feelings.
paper, 64 pages

Unlimit Your Life
by James Fadiman, Ph.D.

How to assess and understand the factors holding you back in life, and then set concrete goals and start working towards attaining them in the most effective, life-affirming fashion.
paper, 224 pages

Love is Letting Go of Fear
by Gerald Jampolsky, M.D.

The lessons in this extremely popular little book (over 1,000,000 in print), based on A Course in Miracles, will teach you to let go of fear and remember that our true essence is love. Includes daily exercises.
paper or cloth, 160 pages

To order please write:
Celestial Arts
P.O. Box 7123, Berkeley, California 94707
Or call (800) 841-BOOK.